БАЛИ

How to use this book

Following the tradition established by Karl Baedeker in 1846, sights of particular interest are distinguished by either one * or two ** stars.

To make it easier to locate the various sights listed in the "A to Z" section of the Guide, their co-ordinates on the large map of Bali are shown in red at the head of each entry.

Only a selection of hotels and restaurants can be given: no reflection is implied, therefore, on establishments not included.

The symbol ⓘ on a town plan indicates the local tourist office from which further information can be obtained. The post-horn symbol indicates a post office.

In a time of rapid change it is difficult to ensure that all the information given is entirely accurate and up to date, and the possibility of error can never be completely eliminated. Although the publishers can accept no responsibility for inaccuracies and omissions, they are always grateful for corrections and suggestions for improvement.

Preface

This guide to Bali is one of the new generation of Baedeker guides.

These guides, illustrated throughout in colour, are designed to meet the needs of the modern traveller. They are quick and easy to consult, with the principal places of interest described in alphabetical order, and the information is presented in a format that is both attractive and easy to follow.

This guide covers the Indonesian island of Bali in the Lesser Sunda Islands together with its smaller subsidiary islands, and also includes the neighbouring island of Lombok to the east.

The guide is in three parts. The first part gives a general account of Indonesia, and in particular of Bali – its topography, climate, flora and fauna, protection of nature and the environment, population, religion, government and administration, economy, history, famous people, art and culture. A selection of literary quotations and some suggested itineraries lead into the second part, in which places of tourist interest are described. The third part contains a variety of practical information. Both the sights and the practical information are listed in alphabetical order.

Artistic layout of the rice terraces shape the landscape of the Indonesian island of Bali

The new Baedeker guides are noted for their concentration on essentials and their convenience of use. They contain numerous specially drawn plans and colour illustrations; and at the end of the book is a large map making it easy to locate the various places described in the "A to Z" section of the guide with the help of the co-ordinates given at the head of each entry.

Contents

Nature, Culture, History
Pages 10–76

Sights from A to Z
Pages 77–151

Practical Information from A to Z
Pages 153–208

Baedeker Specials

Gods, Ghosts

Once a year something very strange happens on Sanur beach not far from Denpasar, the capital of Bali: thousands of people simply sit there, just a few yards from the gently breaking waves, of the infinite sea. They gaze at the slowly receding waters of the ebb tide and the rapidly sinking sun. From time to time they turn their heads in the direction of the small altar, crowned with a baldachin, on which two figures with shaggy horse-like hair sit together in peaceful harmony. Suddenly there is movement: when the glare of the sun eases and the crowd has been increased, probably for the last time, by the arrival of a further hundred or so people dressed in white and yellow, the first of them stand up and walk towards the sea. In their hands they carry small boats of woven palm leaves containing a little rice, a few coins and some tropical flower blossoms: blue ones for Wishnu, red for Brahma and white for Shiva – the three most important deities of Hinduism. The wet sand preserves their foot prints until the next gentle wave arrives and the water collects for a moment in their tracks. As if given a sign, they lay the boats on the sand, freeze for a moment in quiet devotion and return and sit down in their places.

However, and this also forms part of the scene, among all these many hundreds of devotees tourists in sweaty batik shirts stalk around with rolled-up trouser legs. Their thumbs resting on the red start

Odalan
is the "birthday" of a Balinese temple to which the women bring artistic offerings

The Pura Besakih:
the most important temple celebrations take place here every hundred years

Natural Happiness
is an indispensable component of life on Bali

and Demons

uttons of ever ready video cameras. If something unusual happens on the
beach they become slightly agitated, operate this or that button and press the
rubber eyepieces of their viewfinders tightly to their eyes. "What are they
doing there?", asks someone for whom the activities of the locals are not
immediately clear. "I don't know", whispers an elderly American man in a red-
blue checked hat. It is the evening before Nyepi, the Balinese new year, when
believers gather on Sanur beach to pray for the benevolence of the sea spirits during the coming year. Gods, ghosts and demons – mysterious creatures
between heaven and earth – become
almost tangible on Bali. But tangible only
for those who take the trouble to learn
something of Balinese culture and
religion.

The serious economic crisis which has
gripped all the tiger economies since
1997 can be felt on Bali just as everywhere else in Indonesia. But the starting
position is different here: though
Muslims form the majority in the rest of
Indonesia, Bali is primarily Hindu. The
radical change championed by the
Muslim fundamentalists, which they will
bring about by force if necessary,
will therefore probably never occur on
Bali. After a short breathing space, the
number of visitors to Bali is clearly
increasing again. Perhaps Bali is indeed
the island of the gods, a peaceful refuge
in a turbulent world.

Temples

*on Bali are
characterized by
detailed shapes
and express the
high artistic skill of
the islanders*

Harmony

*between man and nature is
expressed by Balinese
architecture. A good example is
Puri Anyar, the former princely
residence in Karambitan, now a
hotel*

Nature, Culture History

Facts and Figures

General

Indonesia (the "Indian island world"), the third largest state in Asia (after China and India), occupies the main part of the Malay Archipelago, between the Indian Ocean and the Pacific, and has also annexed the western half of the island of New Guinea.

The islands of Indonesia, numbering over 13,670 in all, only some 350 of them with an area of more than 100sq. km (39 sq. mi.) and less than half of them inhabited, lie on both sides of the Equator between latitude 6°8′ north and 11°15′ south and between longitude 94°15′ and 141°5′ east.

Indonesia thus extends for almost 1890 km (1175 mi.) from north to south and for some 5100 km (3170 mi.) from east to west. It covers a total area, on land and water, of around 5.2 million sq. km (2 million sq. mi.), with a total land area of just under 2 million sq. km (775,000 sq. mi.).

The largest islands in the Indonesian archipelago are the Greater Sunda Islands of Sumatra, Java, Kalimantan (Borneo; most of it belonging to Indonesia) and Sulawesi (Celebes), the Lesser Sunda Islands of Bali, Lombok, Sumbawa, Sumba, Flores, Timor, etc., and the Moluccas (the Maluku group, formerly known as the Spice Islands).

The Indonesian annexation of Irian Jaya, the western part (area 422,000 sq. km (163,000 sq. mi.) of the island of New Guinea, and of the former Portuguese colonial territory of East Timor (15,000 sq. km (5800 sq. mi.) attracted international criticism.

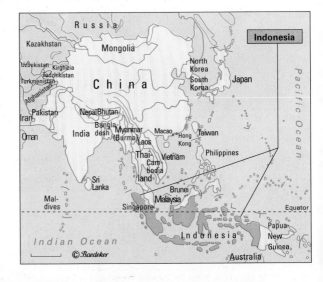

◄ *The Legong Dance, only performed by very young girls, in which the "language of the hands and fingers" plays an important part*

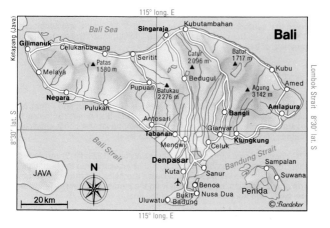

Indonesia's nearest neighbours are Malaysia (Kalimantan/Borneo) to the north and Papua-New Guinea to the east.

Bali, the most westerly of the Lesser Sunda Islands, is probably the best known island in the Indonesian Archipelago as far as tourists are concerned. Its unique character has fascinated Bali visitors since time immemorial. Here, in contrast to the rest of Indonesia, Hinduism has maintained its position vis-a-vis Islam. A luxuriant tropical vegetation, artistically arranged rice terraces, numerous shrines, rich arts and crafts, colourful markets and the famous temple dances exert a magical attraction throughout the year on holiday makers from all over the world. | Bali

The natives of the island do not call it Bali: to them it is Nusa Dua, the Great Island. | Name

Bali lies in latitude 8°30' north and longitude 115° east, washed on the north by the Bali Sea (Indonesian name Laut Bali) and on the south by the Indian Ocean (this part of which is known in Indonesian as Samudera Indonesia). | Geographical situation

It is separated from Java, to the west, by the Bali Strait (Selat Bali), an arm of the sea which at its narrowest point is only 2.5 km (1½ mi.) wide, and from its smaller eastern neighbour, the island of Lombok, by the 40 km (25 mi.) wide Lombok Strait (Selat Lombok).

With an area of 5501 sq. km (2124 sq. mi.), Bali is more than twice the size of the Grand Duchy of Luxembourg (2586 sq. km (998 sq. mi.)). Its maximum length from west to east is 145 km (90 mi.), its maximum width from north to south 95 km (60 mi.). | Area

Included within the province of Bali (area 5561 sq. km (2147 sq. mi.)) are the offshore islands of Nusa Penida (the largest), Nusa Cemingan and Nusa Lembongan, which are separated from the main island by the Badung Strait (Selat Badung), and the little island of Pulau Serangan | Subsidiary islands

(Turtle Island), which closes off Benoa Bay at the southern tip of Bali. Off the north-western tip of Bali is the uninhabited islet of Pulau Mejangan.

The capital: Denpasar

Near the southern tip of Bali, in latitude 8°39′ south and longitude 115°13′ east, is Denpasar, the chief town and administrative centre of the province of Bali.

Geography

Origin

Bali was not always an island: until about 10,000 years ago – that is, before the last ice age – it was linked with Java, Borneo and Sumatra. It was transformed into an island by the melting of the continental ice masses and the accompanying rise in sea level.

Wallace Line

The great British zoologist Alfred Russel Wallace (1823–1913) concluded that the Lombok Strait between Bali and Lombok marked the boundary, now known as the Wallace Line, between the Asian and the Australasian continental shelves, basing his view on the marked differences between the fauna and flora on either side of the line.

Highest peaks

The highest points on Bali are the volcanoes of Agung (3142 m (10,309 ft)) and Batukau (2276 m (7468 ft)).
The highest point on Lombok is the volcano of Rinjani (3726 m (12,225 ft)).

Rivers

Almost all Bali's rivers and streams, rising mainly in the centre of the island, flow either north or south, with an abundant supply of water which feeds an intricate network of irrigation canals.

Volcanism

The geology of many Indonesian islands is characterised by numerous volcanoes, not a few of which are still active. This is the case also with Bali and Lombok.

Volcanoes are found, and are still being formed, at weak spots on the earth's crust, which may lie as much as several thousand metres below sea level but may on occasion (like the San Andreas fault in California) be visible on the surface. Although with present methods of monitoring it is relatively easy to locate incidents of volcanic activity, usually accompanying earthquakes, the occurrence of eruptions cannot readily be forecast, and they thus present a latent threat to the inhabitants of vulnerable areas. Deep within a volcano is a region of extraordinarily high pressures and high temperature, and the eruptions which result from the discharge of gas under high pressure normally take place at the weakest spot in the earth's crust: that is, usually in the volcanic cone formed by earlier eruptions. In an eruption molten rock (magma) is hurled out of the vent, and the resultant stream of lava then flows downhill, carrying with it everything that lies in its way, until finally it cools down and solidifies, leaving in its wake a newly created and often bizarrely shaped landscape.

Gunung Agung – Bali's highest mountain

No less destructive of all life than the lava is the volcanic ash which pours down on the earth in a red-hot rain; but although it destroys the vegetation for the time being it breaks down in course of time into a fertilising ingredient which improves the quality of the soil.

A volcanic landscape is, typically, much broken up and dissected as a result of the varying force and intensity of the lava flows. In the course of centuries this may result in an inversion of the relief pattern, when areas which were originally depressions are transformed by the erosion of the surrounding slopes into high ground or even into considerable hills.

Topography

The centre of Bali is dominated by four separate volcanic complexes, the highest of which is Gunung Agung (3142 m (10,309 ft)), near the east end of the island. North-west of this is Gunung Batur (1717 m (5633 ft)), with a large crater lake.

Central Bali

Farther west are Catur (2096 m (6877 ft)) and Batukau (2276 m (7468 ft)). These mighty volcanic complexes form a giant inverted V with its open end towards the island's chief town, Denpasar.

Southern Bali is the most fertile part of the island. It is a region of well watered alluvial plains fertilised by volcanic ash lying on the windward side of the central volcanic hills. They have high rainfall throughout the year, providing an abundant supply of water for irrigation. This is the most intensively cultivated part of the island, with extensive terraced rice-fields.

South Bali

The narrow western end of the island is an area of deep valleys between

West Bali

Terraced rice-fields on Bali

ranges of hills which came into being in the Tertiary era (National Park). Lying in the lee of the hills, it is considerably drier than the southern part of the island.

East Bali

The mountain ranges of central Bali reach close to the east coast of the island and determine the topography of this area. The dominant features are Gunung Agung, whose central cone and foothills extending north and south set the pattern of the landscape, and Gunung Batur, which forms a transition to central Bali.

Climate

Seasons

By the standards of South-East Asia Bali has an unusually settled climate. There are only two seasons, a dry period from April to October and a rainy period from November to March. This pattern is influenced by factors originating on the Australian continent.

Rainfall

From November onwards there are frequent high winds from Australia which pick up moisture over the sea and reach Indonesia as the monsoon. This produces falls of rain in Bali which are sometimes heavy, reaching a maximum in January, with an average of 326 mm (13 in.) at Denpasar. The lowest rainfall is in August, with 34 mm (1.3 in.), when hot, dry winds blow from the north. But even in winter it can happen that southern Bali has cloudless skies, while elsewhere it may rain all day without interruption.

Weather stn Denpasar (alt. 1m/3ft) Source: German Weather Service Hamburg Months	Rainfall in mm/in.	Days with rain (≥1mm/day)	Max. day temperature in °C/°F	Min. night temperature in °C/°F	Water temperature in °C/°F	Sunshine (hours per day)	Relative air humidity (%)
			Climatic Table for Bali				
January	326/12.8	16	31.0/87.8	23.7/74.7	28/82	5.2	78
February	325/12.8	15	31.1/88.0	23.7/74.7	28/82	5.1	80
March	209/8.2	13	31.2/88.2	23.5/74.3	28/82	5.4	78
April	84/3.3	6	31.6/88.9	23.2/73.8	29/84	6.9	78
May	78/3.1	5	31.2/88.2	23.2/73.8	28/82	6.7	79
June	72/2.8	5	30.4/86.7	22.4/72.3	28/82	6.6	79
July	61/2.4	4	29.7/85.5	22.4/72.3	28/82	6.9	77
August	34/1.3	3	29.9/85.8	22.3/72.1	27/81	7.4	75
September	54/2.1	3	30.6/87.1	22.6/72.7	27/81	6.9	75
October	110/4.3	5	31.4/88.5	23.3/73.9	27/81	7.1	75
November	191/7.5	8	31.5/88.7	23.6/74.5	28/82	6.1	76
December	293/11.5	14	31.2/88.2	23.6/74.5	29/84	5.8	79
Year	1837/72.3	96	30.9/87.6	23.1/73.6	28/82	6.3	77

Average day temperatures show little variation over the year. On the coast and on low ground in the interior of the island they range between 29.7°C (85.5°F) and 31.6°C (88.9°F) over the year; but, with cool breezes blowing in constantly from the sea, it is never unpleasantly hot. In the upland regions temperatures are on average about 5°C (9°F) lower, and in the early morning the difference can be even greater. In the lowlands temperatures at night may be anything up to 8°C (14.4°F) lower.

The temperature of the sea remains almost constantly warm throughout the year. The average water temperature is around 27.9°C (82.2°F) in April, and in December may be as high as 29°C (84.2°F).

Temperatures

Between April and October there are on average between 6.9 and 7.5 hours of sunshine a day. During the rest of the year, when the sky is sometimes clouded over, the duration of sunshine may be up to 2 hours less.

Sunshine

What may sometimes trouble visitors from temperate regions is the relatively high humidity of the air. This may rise in February as high as 80 per cent, and falls in August and September by only about 5 per cent. Those who would feel uncomfortable in conditions of high humidity should visit Bali between May/June and September/October, since during the rest of the year, with high air temperatures, it can be almost intolerably sultry.

Humidity

Flora and Fauna

Flora

Scarcely any other island in the Indonesian archipelago is so intensively cultivated as Bali. Rice-fields extend as far as the eye can reach, and every patch of earth, however small, is used to produce up to two rice harvests a year.

There is, however, another Bali, mainly to be found in the western part of the island, and specifically in the Bali Barat National Park: a region of tropical jungle, consisting of fine woods such as mahogany at the lower levels and of tall, slender pines and various dipterocarpaceous species (trees with two-winged fruits). In the south there are extensive forests of palms, which in the gently rising country towards the centre of the island give place to rice-fields of greater or lesser size. In contrast to the harmonious landscapes of these areas the southern coastal region – a marshy, brackish transitional zone between land and sea – may at first sight appear less attractive. In eastern Bali, on the other hand, where the mountains reach down close to the coast, there are still areas suitable for agricultural development.

In the upland regions the flora becomes sparser. Here the characteristic vegetation consists of tough, low-growing shrubs and plants, which at the higher levels almost completely disappear, giving place to a barren region of black lava rock with little vegetation of any kind.

The mighty banyan (Sanskrit *nyagrodha*), a species of fig-tree characteristic of South-East Asia, is regarded as a sacred tree. The banyan found on Bali is *Ficus bengalensis*, which can reach a height of 30 m (100 ft), with a wide spreading crown whose branches are supported on aerial roots. Since banyans drive out other trees they are rarely found in isolation but form whole forests. The banyan is particularly venerated because it was under one such tree in southern India that Siddharta Gautama is believed to have attained Enlightenment and to have subsequently been admitted to Nirvana as the first Buddha. Almost every village on Bali has a banyan tree, and often more than one.

The banyan

Secondary forest replacing cleared jungle

Useful plants

Bali has a rich flora, but one which primarily serves to provide the population with food. There are large plantations of pineapples, bananas, vegetables, coffee, coconuts and betel nuts. Betel nuts are particularly popular with older people as an aphrodisiac drug. Small pieces of the not-quite-ripe nut are wrapped in leaves of the betel pepper which have been smeared with lime and are then chewed. The advantage of the betel nut as a drug is that it has a stimulating effect and produces a feeling of wellbeing without interfering with the user's capacity for work. A disadvantage is that with frequent use it stains the teeth, saliva and lips red and may sometimes produce chronic inflammations in the mouth.

Balinese coffee is an important export, but tea, tobacco and spices are of relatively little consequence: only small quantities are grown and are confined to the local market. Of great importance are the coconut palm and the fast-growing bamboo, both of which are used as building material. Orchids are rarer on Bali than in other parts of South-East Asia, but the lotus is commonly found.

Fauna

Terrestrial fauna

Bali's terrestrial fauna is as abundant as its flora. The Bengal tiger, of which in the past there were large numbers on Bali, appears now to be extinct on the island: at any rate none have been seen for many years. Among animals still found on Bali are some smaller species of crocodile, monitors, iguanas and tortoises. There are also, particularly in the jungle regions, various species of snakes, some of them venomous.

The forests of Bali are home to large numbers of monkeys and tropical birds, including various species of parrots and finches. Bali is also the last refuge of the Bali starling (*Leucopsar Rothschildi*), now threatened with extinction (with an estimated population of only some 200)

Monkeys on Bali – sometimes cheeky and aggressive

and therefore strictly protected: a bird some 25 cm (10 in.) long, white apart from blue patches round the eyes and black tips to its wings and tail. Bats and flying foxes are revered as sacred.

A charming and entirely harmless animal frequently seen on Bali, particularly in the evening and during the night, is the gecko (*tokeh*), a South-East Asian member of the lizard family, which performs a useful function in catching insects. Geckos tend to gather in groups around lights, chattering noisily but disappearing at once when approached.

Geckos

The stolid water-buffalo is much in use both as a draught animal and in the cultivation of the rice-fields. Other domesticated animals are the sway-back pigs, the Bali cows (*banteng*), a species related to wild cattle, the ducks which forage in the rice-fields, geese and hens. Large numbers of pigs are kept on Bali; but since the rest of Indonesia is Muslim the island's sucking pigs and pork are exported to Hong Kong.

Working and domestic animals

The seas around Bali are well supplied with fish, mainly tunny and bass. The Balinese, however, are not great fishermen, since they believe that the sea is the home of evil spirits and demons. One sea creature is revered as sacred: the black-and-white striped sea-snake.

Marine fauna

Environment

It is only in quite recent years that there has been serious concern on Bali about the protection of the environment, but the problems – created in part by the great influx of tourists – have now become all too evident. Even the most unobservant visitor walking about Denpasar, for example, cannot fail to notice the contrast between the concern of the Balinese, like other Asian peoples, for cleanliness and hygiene in their personal life and their indifference to the piles of rubbish which accumulate in the streets and the broken glass which litters the beaches. In the absence of any organised system of waste disposal rubbish is merely deposited on casual dumps and set on fire, while sewage is piped into the sea. Government campaigns against these practices have so far had little effect. In areas frequented by tourists, at any rate, some rubbish bins have been installed – imposing a special duty on visitors to set a good example by depositing their rubbish in them.

Road traffic	The problems created by the steadily increasing motor traffic on Bali are equally evident. The pleasure of a walk through Denpasar, for example, is likely to be spoiled by dense clouds of exhaust gases – a situation aggravated by the practice of leaving the engine running when a vehicle is not moving.
Growth of population	A less immediately obvious problem is created by the steadily increasing population of the island. Large families of a dozen or more children are the rule rather than the exception on Bali; and in order to feed them the natural forests are increasingly being cleared and converted to agricultural use.
Soil erosion	One of the most unfortunate, and usually unconsidered, consequences is increasing erosion of the soil; and the forest is now less effective as a factor contributing to an equable climate. Fortunately, however, Bali has so far been spared devastating floods and other natural catastrophes, apart from the occasional volcanic eruptions.
Future prospects	If official statements are to be believed, the Indonesian government is at present engaged in a review of policy which may lead to a greater concern with the protection of nature and the environment. A central feature is likely to be the education of the Balinese population in the proper disposal of waste.

Population

Origins	Indonesia is a land of many different peoples – as is shown by the large number of languages and dialects (over 250) spoken in the islands. The majority of the population, however, belong to the Malayo-Polynesian (Austronesian) family of peoples, often referred to as the Proto-Malays. Bali, like other Indonesian islands, was originally occupied by nomadic peoples. A sharp increase in population began about 3000 B.C., when some peoples living in southern China left their homeland and spread over much of South-East Asia. In the course of this migration, the scale of which it is now difficult to determine, those peoples who were accustomed to sailing on the open sea arrived in the Indonesian archipelago. Their life was closely bound up with nature, they believed in various spirits, demons and gods and they worshipped their ancestors; and something of these religious beliefs can still be found among the present-day Balinese.

Shortly before the beginning of the Christian era there was a further great wave of immigration: the peoples known as the Deutero-Malays, who gradually became completely absorbed into the older population.

Other peoples (e.g. Chinese) who have settled on Bali and its neighbouring islands have remained minorities.

Numbers and density	Bali has a population of some 3 million, with an average density of around 505 inhabitants to the sq. kilometre (1308 to the sq. mile).

People of Bali

As a result of a birth control programme promoted by the Indonesian government, under the slogan "Dua anak cupuk" ("Two children are enough"), the annual rate of population growth has been held down to about 22 per 1000. The problem, however, is that in Balinese society it is essential to have a male descendant, mainly in order to take over the father's religious obligations. In consequence the rapid growth of the population continues, and within the foreseeable future Bali is likely to become over-populated and Balinese agriculture incapable of feeding the island's population.

Growth rate

A further problem now confronting Bali is a tendency towards a drift of population away from the land. Increasing numbers of people are moving into the Denpasar area, the main tourist centre, where they see prospects of earning more money than in their home district.

Flight from the land

Language

Indonesia is a country of many peoples and of more than 250 languages and dialects. Among them is Balinese, which is spoken on Bali and in the western part of the neighbouring island of Lombok. It is one of the Malayo-Polynesian (Austronesian) languages, closely related to Javanese and Sundanese. The Balinese language, however, is steadily being displaced by the language known as Bahasa Indonesia.

Bahasa Indonesia

Bahasa Indonesia, the official language of Indonesia, also belongs to the Malayo-Polynesian language family, but it came into being in its present form only in 1928. It is basically the Malay language, incorporating words from many other languages. A further language reform in 1972 brought about further unification.

Alphabet

Bahasa Indonesia is written in the Latin alphabet, with no diacritics.

Alongside the official language, Bahasa Indonesia, English is widely spoken. English-speaking visitors, therefore, should have no linguistic difficulties.

Education

Schools

Since 1984 Bali, like the rest of Indonesia, has had a six-year period of compulsory school attendance, starting between the ages of six and eight, after which children qualified to do so can go on to secondary education. State education is free of charge.

The establishment of an educational structure based on the primary school and laying increased emphasis on vocational training is planned and has been partly brought into effect. It is hoped, with the help of loans from the World Bank, to extend this system to the whole of Indonesia.

Higher education

Denpasar has a University and two polytechnics. For young people who want to go beyond this there are the higher educational establishments in the Indonesian capital, Jakarta; some go on to study abroad.

Illiteracy

Increased enforcement of the requirement of compulsory school attendance has led to a considerable reduction in illiteracy, which in 1971 was still as high as 40 per cent in rural areas.

Health

Health services on Bali are still at a very modest level. In recent years there has been a considerable increase in the number of general practitioners, but the island's only hospitals are in Denpasar. Even there they are very sparsely equipped, though capable at any rate of providing primary medical care. Outside Denpasar there are state-run health centres (*puskemas*) and medical outpatient departments which can treat common illnesses and minor injuries. The cost of treatment is met by the state, but medicines must be paid for.

Emergency treatment

Bali is not equipped, however, to deal with serious illnesses or injuries. Such cases are usually transferred to Jakarta; for foreign visitors there is also the possibility of transfer to Singapore. There is no ambulance service on the western model on Bali, and in the event of an accident, particularly in the interior of the island, there may be a long wait for any kind of ambulance transport.

Cholera

Cholera is still widely prevalent in Indonesia, and tetanus still takes a leading place among causes of death.

Religion

An estimated 95 per cent of the population of Bali are Hindus; other religions, Buddhism, Islam and Christianity, play only a minor role. In the course of time, however, some Buddhist elements found their way into the Hindu-Balinese religion (Agama Hindu Dharma). Hinduism came to Bali by a relatively direct route, by way of Java, in the first century A.D. In general Balinese Hinduism differs only marginally from its Indian prototype, though it has a much less rigid caste system (see p. 23).

Hinduism

Hinduism is one of the four great world religions, with some 645 million adherents. The name of Hinduism arose from the translation of the Sanskrit word "Indu" into the Iranian "Hindu", and was originally applied only to people living on the river Indus. The use of the term Hinduism for their religious beliefs was a western invention.

In contrast to the monotheistic belief in a single divine person, Indian Hinduism is a monistic religion centred on a depersonalised principle (cf. Buddhism, Confucianism and Taoism). In recent decades, however, there has been a growing school of thought on Bali which has drawn visibly closer to monotheism, worshipping a god with whom all things began – Sangyang Widi, the "all-encompassing god".

The basic ideas of Hinduism have developed over millennia; it does not, however, represent any rigid religious principle. One of the prime elements which are still essential constituents of Hinduism is Brahmanism, which came into being in the 1st century A.D. and drew its basic ideas from Vedism, a religion of ancient India.

The holiest temple of Bali: Pura Besakih

Religion

The eternal cycle

What, then, are the beliefs of a Hindu, who as a human being occupies a middle position on the symbolic ladder of existence? His prime belief is in the never-ending cycle of the birth, death and rebirth of the soul (Samsara) from which no living creature can escape unless after many lives, the number of which cannot be known in advance, he secures admission to Nirvana. In what form the soul of a Hindu will be reborn cannot be determined: he may have another existence as a human being, but he may equally be an animal or a plant, a celestial or an infernal being. Man can, however, influence the cycle by good or evil deeds (Karma), which in his next life will be rewarded or punished by a better or a worse existence. The aim of every Hindu, however, is not to be reborn but to enter Nirvana and thus finally break out of the eternal cycle of birth, death and rebirth.

Three Ways to Salvation

In order to achieve this aim it is important to follow the "Three Ways to Salvation" (Tiga Marga). The first of these Ways involves sacrifices to gods and demons and their varied manifestations; the second consists of the striving towards knowledge and understanding and respect for other men, particularly priests and the old; while the third seeks through self-examination (meditation) to achieve release from man's imprisonment within the five elements, which can be achieved only by union with the divine principle.

Cosmology

The Hindu also has a fairly clear image of the cosmos, based both on mythological and philosophical conceptions and on the simple observation of natural processes. The world, formed from primal matter (*prakriti*), is seen as being caught in a never-ending cycle of development and annihilation, separated from one another by a phase of persistence in a state of rest. Man sees himself as a little world (*buwana alit*) within a great world (*buwana agung*); he is thus himself a part of the macrocosm.

Hindus on the way to and from the temple

KAJA
(north: to mountain)

Vishnu

Sankara   Sambu

KAUH (west)

Mahadevi   Shiva   Ishvara

KANGIN (east)

Mahe-
shvara

Rudra

Brahma

KELOD
(south: to sea)

Padma

The symbol of the religious beliefs of Balinese Hinduism is the lotus blossom (*Nelumbo*), the form of which is seen as an image of the world.

More commonly represented on Bali than the four-leaved lotus (*panca dewata*) is the eight-leaved form (*padma*). In the centre is the god Shiva, surrounded clockwise by the eight gods of the directions – Vishnu, Sambu, Ishvara, Maheshvara, Brahma, Rudra, Mahadevi and San(g)kara.

To these divinities are attributed, along with many other qualities and significances, various colours, characteristics and organs of the body. Four of them represent the four cardinal points – Vishnu the north (Kaja), Brahma the south (Kelod), Mahadevi the west (Kauh) and Ishvara the east (Kangin).

The lotus blossom as a symbol of the Hindu Balinese religion is found in many forms on Bali – carved in stone or as one of the principal elements in traditional batik art.

Each individual belongs from birth to a caste (Indian *varna*). To change from one caste to another is possible only through the process of rebirth; that is, in the next life.

Castes

Although the origin and meaning of the caste system are still obscure, it is supposed that the members of the first castes were concerned to preserve their ethnic, cultural and social traditions within a fixed unit (the tribe or village) undisturbed by influences from outside. There were originally only four castes – the Brahmans (priests), the Ksatrias (warriors), the Wesyas (peasants and craftsmen) and the Sudras (servants) – but in the course of centuries, as a result of mixed marriages and the inclusion of persons not belonging to any caste there developed a complex system which gradually displaced the traditional division.

Those who did not belong to one of the four castes were regarded in India as pariahs, as untouchables; but this distinction was not adopted by the Balinese. On Bali there are only the four main castes, and it is possible in theory to marry into a different caste, though this may give rise to some difficulties.

The traditional high respect accorded to the Brahmans is still maintained – mainly because princes, intellectuals and officials belong to this caste.

There are now said to be some 3000 different castes in India. Even Gandhi (himself a member of the Wesya caste) was unable to prevent the establishment of numerous new castes.

There are no sacred animals in Bali like the sacred cows of India, and there is no ban on the eating of beef, except for Brahmans.

Sacred animals

Hindu Pantheon

In Hindu belief all living things – plants, animals, human beings – have their fixed place on the ladder of existence. On the highest level are the divinities who occupy the temple of the gods (the Pantheon) on Meru,

Belief Built in Stone

The small boy stood in the doorway, smiled and said, with an inviting gesture: "Come in, Mister! Please come in!" He stood aside, leaving room for us to pass through the narrow entrance into his parents' compound. The entrance to any Balinese family compound is made as narrow as possible, and immediately behind it is another obstacle in the form of a low wall. The narrow entrance and the protective wall are important elements in the structure, for outside them evil spirits, demons and other terrifying figures lie in wait. If uninvited guests of this kind cannot be entirely driven away they can at least be kept outside.

Belief built in stone: that is perhaps the best explanation of the layout of a traditional Balinese farmstead. The compound (*kampong*) consists of a number of buildings (*bale*) of varying size surrounded by a solid outer wall. The wall not only serves to ward off unwanted, invisible visitors but is also the visible symbol of the cohesion and solidarity of the Balinese extended family.

The uninitiated observer may be puzzled by the unchanging uniformity. In a Balinese village compound after compound is the same. All the entrances are on the same side; within the rectangular enclosure the inevitable family temple is always in the same position; and the various separate buildings are arranged in almost exactly the same pattern. At first sight it is difficult to see any real difference between one compound and another. Whether the family is rich or poor, the family temple, the living and the sleeping apartments, the kitchen, the rice store, the stalls for the domestic animals and a building which serves various ritual purposes are laid out on broadly the same plan. Only one feature distinguishes a family of higher social rank: the more prosperous Balinese have an additional building in which various ceremonies prescribed by the Hindu religion are performed.

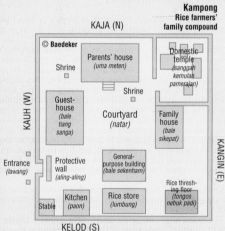

Kampong
Rice farmers'
family compound

The number of buildings containing the living and sleeping apartments varies according to the size of the family. The largest building, always situated close to the family shrine, belongs to the grandparents, who enjoy the greatest respect. The younger generation sleep separately according to sex; sometimes unmarried girls and young women are accommodated in the grandparents' house.
At any rate in the country areas of Bali it is the rule rather than the exception for the whole of the extended family to live under one (symbolic) roof. It is not uncommon to find three or even four generations living in the same compound. When a girl marries the young couple move in with the parents of the bridegroom.

the world mountain; and below them are holy men, kings, spirits and demons.

There are large numbers of gods and other divinities, headed by the Trinity (Trimurti) of Brahma, Vishnu and Shiva. They can take on any form they please: they can visit Bali in the body of any creature or object, of which they take temporary possession.

There is one important difference between the traditional Hinduism of India and that professed by most believers on Bali with its monotheistic trend: they believe in Sangyang Widi, a god who carries within him the all-embracing divine principle.

Brahma, creator of the world, was originally the supreme god of   Brahma

Gods, spirits and demons play an important part in the life of the Balinese

25

Hinduism. He now has roughly the same status as Shiva and Vishnu, with whom he forms the Divine Trinity (Trimurti).

Vishnu

Vishnu is the sustainer of the world, who took on human form as Krishna.

Shiva

Shiva is the destroyer and dissolver of the world. On Bali one of his numerous manifestations is known as Sangyang Guru. Shiva is frequently represented in the form of a lingam (phallic symbol).

Consorts of the gods

The wives of Brahma, Vishnu and Shiva are Sarasvati, Lakshmi and Shakti, who stand symbolically for learning, good fortune and power.

Sangyang Widi

Sangyang Widi is the supreme god of Balinese Hinduism, representing the incarnation of the three principal gods (Brahma, Vishnu and Shiva) and thus symbolising the all-embracing divine principle.

Dewi Sri

Dewi Sri is one of the principal goddesses in Balinese Hinduism. Her name, of Sanskrit origin, means "goddess of splendour". As the rice goddess, she takes on the shape of grains of rice (Nini) at the time of the first rice harvest, and in this form is revered as an incarnation of Shiva.

Dewi Danu

Dewi Danu is another important goddess. Her main sphere of influence is Lake Batur, but she is also revered as the mistress of the other lakes on the island.

Dewa Sedana and Dewi

Two of the numerous manifestations of Vishnu are the god Dewa Sedana and his consort Dewi. They are revered as god and goddess of prosperity and wealth and accordingly are particularly welcome visitors to temple festivals.

Lesser gods

Lower in the hierarchy are the gods associated with natural events and natural forces, like Indra (rain), Surya (the sun), Soma (the moon), Vayu (wind), Agni (fire), Varuna (the waters), Yama (death), Kama (love), Kubera (wealth), Skanda (war) and Ganesha (the removal of obstacles).

Lower gods

Among the numerous gods still lower in the divine hierarchy are some who intervene to a greater or lesser extent in the life of the world, either for good or for evil.

Spirits and demons

The lowest rank in the system of Hinduism, far below the gods and other divinities, is occupied by a numerous array of spirits and demons.

Although spirits and demons are in general unloved beings, some of them have the important task of keeping still more evil spirits away from the precincts of temples.

Religious practices

Festivals

On Bali there are a great variety of religious practices, which nevertheless have one thing in common: they all provide a welcome occasion for a festival, which may be celebrated either within the family or, more usually, with the other inhabitants of the village.

Rites of passage

Particularly important in the life of the Balinese are the rituals, usually of Hindu origin, performed before or after the passage from one stage of life to the next. Strictly speaking, the passage out of one phase of life into the next is a "little death" and the entry into the next phase a "little rebirth". The rites of passage between the different phases of life are known to the Balinese as *manusa yadnya*.

In the early months of a woman's pregnancy various ceremonies are
performed with the object of warding off evil spirits from the child and
inducing good spirits to enter its body. An important part is played by
offerings in the temples, which may be made only by close relatives.
During her pregnancy the mother is regarded as impure and may not
enter a temple or a rice-field.

When the child is born its "four companions" (*kanda mpat*: amniotic
fluid, placenta, umbilical cord and blood) must be buried in a painted
coconut shell at the entrance to the sleeping-house. A deity called Rare
Kumara watches over the child's bed and has a special shrine next to it.
Ribbons and small chains are tied round the child's wrists and ankles to
ward off evil spirits.

On the 12th and the 42nd day after the birth there are further ceremonies, of Brahmanist origin, to purify the mother and child.

Until the 210th day (the child's first "birthday" according to the
Balinese calendar) it must always be carried about and never allowed to
touch the ground. On that day there is a great celebration during which
the child is symbolically set on the ground and thus officially crosses the
boundary between divine transcendence and earthly existence; and the
child and its four companions are given new names in order to confuse
the spirits.

On reaching puberty both boys and girls must undergo the ceremony of
tooth-filing, after which they are regarded as of marriageable age. The
ceremony is performed by a Brahman priest, who files down to a
straight line the four upper incisors and the two canines, which belong
to the gods, but leaves the lower teeth as they are, since they belong to
the demons. The filing of the teeth eliminates the six evils (greed, jeal-
ousy, stupidity, lust, anger and lack of control) which may be tolerated in
a child but not in an adult.

The tooth-filing ceremony is a very painful one, but it is regarded as
an event of great importance in the life of a Hindu believer which must
be endured. In many parts of Bali, however, the tooth-filing is now performed only symbolically.

Circumcision is practised only on the sons of Muslim parents, particularly on the neighbouring island of Lombok. Some ethnologists believe
that the tooth-filing ceremony serves a similar function.

When he marries a Balinese man assumes the right and the duty to
organise and perform all the rites hitherto carried out by his parents. As
a rule the wife joins her husband in his parents' compound
(*pekarangan*). As a sign that he is now a full member of the community
he takes over from his father responsibility for the wellbeing of the gods
who are worshipped in the family temple. For this purpose the family
gathers at certain fixed intervals during the year in order to perform in
common their exactly prescribed religious duties. On these occasions
members of the family who live elsewhere on Bali return to their home
village.

Death is the most important of the Hindu rites of passage, when the
dead person once again leaves the material world. The body, originally
infused by Brahma with the divine breath, is regarded merely as the
temporary housing of the soul, and after death it dissolves into its five
constituent elements of fire, water, air, earth and ether, which then re-
enter the world of the gods and demons.

There are no cemeteries in the western sense on Bali: the dead are
cremated in accordance with Hindu ritual. In the first stage of the ceremony the body is buried for a period of at least 42 days; there are special
arrangements for Brahman priests, who are embalmed in a manner
which is strictly prescribed and lie on a bier for a period determined by
an astrologer on the basis of complicated calculations. After the 42 days,

and frequently only after the passage of several months or even years, the remains of the dead person are disinterred and prepared for cremation; if little of the body is left a symbolic sandalwood doll is cremated instead. The length of time for which the soul must remain in the body depends on the prosperity of the family. In order to make it easier for the soul to leave the body a bamboo tube is inserted into the grave.

Cremation

The cremation of the dead is the most elaborate and complex of all Balinese ceremonies, for its object is to enable the dead person to enter as easily as possible into another and a better world. Preparations for the event may take weeks or even months.

Three days before the day appointed for the cremation the body is disinterred, purified, wrapped in a shroud and laid, together with various offerings, in a temporary sarcophagus (*bade*), richly decked with flowers, which is then carried in a lively and colourful procession to the place of cremation. This is not an occasion for mourning but a joyous event; for although the death of a close relative may bring sorrow and pain the Balinese live in hope that in his next life the dead person will be born into a better existence – though in Balinese belief this is possible only within the dead person's own family. Behind the temporary sarcophagus is carried the sarcophagus in which the body will be cremated, a pagoda-like structure of anything up to eleven tiers. The sarcophagi are accompanied not only by the relatives of the dead person but usually by almost the whole population of the village. Music is provided by a gamelan orchestra (see Art and Culture, Music), whose strains send the crowd into ecstasy. On the way to the cremation site the bearers of the sarcophagus will suddenly circle round or change direction in order to annoy the spirits. Sometimes the dead man's eldest son sits in one of the lower storeys of the pagoda – a position which in view of the unstable nature of the structure and its violently swaying motion is not without risk.

When the procession arrives at the place of cremation the body is transferred from the temporary sarcophagus to the more elaborate one used for the actual cremation. The form of the sarcophagus indicates the caste to which the dead person belonged. In the case of a Brahman (for example a priest) it is in the form of a bull speckled black and white. If it is in the form of a lion or a stag the dead person belonged to the Jaba or the Wesya caste. For members of the Ksatria caste the sarcophagus is in the form of a bull (black for a man, white for a woman), and it will often be preceded by a magnificent snake or dragon figure.

Members of the Pasek caste have a different type of sarcophagus. While the sarcophagi of the castes already mentioned can rise into the air – in Hindu belief the lion has wings, and the bull is the mount of the god Shiva – the sarcophagus of a member of the Pasek caste is in the form of the elephant fish (*gajah minea*).

Types of sarcophagus

Finally the sarcophagus is set alight and the dead person's soul is borne into the air by the purifying fire. When the body has been consumed the relatives gather up the ashes and any remaining fragments of bone and lay them in a small litter which is then carried in procession to the sea (or to a nearby river), where it is given over to the water.

This is by no means the end of the ritual. At exactly prescribed periods after the cremation there are further elaborate ceremonies which, it is believed, help to purify the dead person's soul of all that is evil or bad.

Cremation

◀ *A Balinese cremation*

An elaborate cremation pagoda ...

... and a smaller one

Temple festivals

Odalan

Every temple on Bali has an annual "birthday festival" (*odalan*) on the anniversary of its first consecration. This is an event in which the whole village takes part, and preparations for it may take weeks or even months. The exact date when the preparation of the offerings can begin, however, must be fixed by a Brahman after complex calculations based on the Javanese/Balinese calendar. The gods are symbolically invited to the festival and as a rule readily accept the invitation, come down from the Pantheon and take the places which have been set aside for them and specially purified in the sacred temple precinct (*bale paruman*), from which they watch over the exact performance of the prescribed rites.

The birthday festival lasts three days, on each of which there are particular ceremonies to be performed.

On the first (and most important) day the gods are received in the temple, which has been elaborately purified and decorated with brightly coloured fabrics, and presented with offerings.

In order that the gods may not be harassed by any demons who may be hovering around the villagers slaughter a pig on the morning of the first day and lay out the meat for the demons at some suitable place.

The Brahman priest then takes a number of small sandalwood figures from the *gedong*, a small closed building in the inner courtyard of the temple, and solemnly carries them to a little pavilion, in which they are set up after being purified in holy water (*tirtha*) and dressed in ceremonial garments.

When the moment of the gods' arrival approaches the priest lights an incense-burner, so that the incense rising into the air may serve as a symbolic ladder from heaven. The gods then begin their descent, to the booming of a gong, and the crowd of worshippers who have come to

Women making a sacrifice on Sanur beach

Women carrying offerings on the way to an odalan festival

the temple with great piles of offerings fall silent in awe and fascination at this supreme moment of the ceremony.

The gods are now ready to receive the reverence that is their due, making use of the priest's help for the purpose. The worshippers are sprinkled with holy water; they take lotus blossoms by the tips of their fingers, raise them three times above their forehead and then drop them. Then follows the symbolic washing of their faces and the upper part of their bodies. Women carry offerings of fruit and other foods, elaborately stacked up, into the temple, where they are received by the priests and symbolically presented to the gods. The offerings are usually collected again in the evening, after the gods have consumed their spiritual essence.

The gods are then able to watch the three days of festival, celebrated in a very relaxed way, with cockfights, shadow plays (*wayang*) and the musical background provided by the gamelan orchestra, all of which is enjoyed both by the gods and by the villagers.

On the second day of the festival the village is purified of all the evil remaining from the past year. On the third day, with the help of the gods, the evil spirits are driven away and the temple and the village are prepared for the new year. In the late evening the gods take their departure and the sandalwood figures are undressed and returned to the *gedong*. The festival ends with the closing of the inner gate of the temple, and the innermost precinct remains inaccessible until the next birthday festival.

Society

Indonesia

At the time this guide went to press, the Indonesian state and society were undergoing a political upheaval which it is difficult to assess. The cause was the grave economic and financial crisis which began in Thailand in 1997 and then gripped the whole of Asia leading to an extremely problematic situation, particularly in the tiger economies. Indonesia especially saw some violent communal disturbances. Though Bali was to a large extent spared, it was nonetheless touched indirectly. Ibrahim Suharto, the head of state and absolute ruler since 1967, lost his office after bloody riots in Jakarta. However, Bacharuddin Jusuf Habibie, his successor, was also unable to solve the country's economic problems and thus to effect a reduction of the tensions between the people and the government. New disturbances, which rocked the Indonesian capital Jakarta in November 1998, caused Habibie to cancel the promised democratic parliamentary elections.

The following statements about the political and social conditions in Indonesia and also on Bali must therefore be read with reservations.

Indonesia, unilaterally proclaimed an independent state on August 17th 1945 (though the Netherlands, the colonial power, recognised its independence only in 1949), is officially designated the Republic of Indonesia (Republik Indonesia).

On the proclamation of its independence Indonesia adopted its national flag (Sang Saka Merah Putih), banded red and white.

National flag

Coat of arms

The Indonesian coat of arms, adopted on February 11th 1950, shows Sang Radja Walik, more commonly known as Garuda, the bird which is Vishnu's mount, with outspread wings, holding a shield with the symbols of the five principles (*panca sila*) of the state: sovereignty and self-defence (a five-pointed star), fight for freedom and cultivation of rice (a water-buffalo's head), national consciousness and unity (a *warigin* tree), social justice (an ear of *pedi* and leaves of the cotton plant) and equality of the sexes (a chain). In its claws the bird holds a scroll with the inscription "Bhinneka tunggal ika" ("Unity in diversity"), derived from a Javanese text of the 15th century.

Indonesia is a centrally organised republic headed by a President (an authoritarian republic with a presidential system).

   The concept of a "guided democracy" introduced by the founder of the state, Sukarno (see Famous People), still prevails in Indonesia. All power rests with the President: the only function of the Parliament is to agree to the legislation put forward by the President.

Form of government

Bacharuddin Jusuf Habibie (born 1936), a qualified aircraft designer, replaced ex-General Ibrahim Suharto as head of state in 1998. Habibie, who took his degree in Germany and was subsequently involved in the development of components for the airbus, was invited to take charge by the military and since then has been regarded as its extended arm.

Head of state

Under the constitution of 1945, as supplemented in 1969, Indonesia is governed by a Consultative Assembly (Madjelis Permusyawaratan Rakyat), which meets only once every five years and elects the President, who is head of the government as well as head of state. The Assembly has 920 members appointed by the provinces and special regions of the country.

   According to several announcements, in future the government will be elected directly by the people in general elections. However, after renewed disturbances the elections promised for the summer of 1999 were cancelled until further notice.

Government

Indonesia's Parliament is the House of Representatives (Dewan Perwakilan Rakyat), which has 460 members, 360 of them elected and 100 appointed by the President.

Parliament

The largest party is Golkar, which is closely associated with the government. Rather than a party in the normal sense it is an alliance of various interest groups (officials, teachers, trade unions). There is no opposition of any consequence. Communist-oriented parties have been banned since 1966.

Parties

Indonesia consists of three Special Regions (*daerah*) and 24 Provinces (*propinsi*), each ruled by a governor (*guvernur*). The provinces are divided into districts (*kabupaten*), each headed by a regent (*bupati*).

Administrative subdivisions (see map p. 34)

Bali

Bali lay within the Javanese sphere of influence from a very early period but gained its independence in the 16th century. During the conversion of Java to Islam (down to the 16th century) it became a place of refuge for Hindus. In the 17th century it gained control of the island of Lombok and the eastern tip of Java. In 1839 it came under Dutch sovereignty, and from 1908 under direct rule by the Netherlands government. From 1942 to 1945 the island was occupied by the Japanese, and in 1946 was granted the special status of an autonomous region. It was the scene of much fighting during the struggle for Indonesian independence, and in 1949, after the Dutch recognition of the new Indonesian state, was incorporated in the Republic of Indonesia as the province of Bali. In 1950 the historic Balinese princedoms which had been re-established in 1938 were dissolved and replaced by administrative districts.

The province of Bali is divided into eight districts (*kabupaten*): Badung (with the provincial capital, Denpasar), Bangli, Buleleng, Gianyar,

Districts

Singaraja

BULELENG

BANGLI

JEMBRANA

Negara

KARANGASEM

TABANAN

Bangli

Amlapura

GIAN-
YAR

ADMINISTRATIVE DISTRICTS
KAPUBATEN
(formerly princedoms)

Tabanan

Klung-
kung

BA-
DUNG
Denpasar

Gianyar

KLUNGKUNG

© *Baedeker*

— Boundaries of districts
● Chief town of district
● Chief town of province

Jembrana, Karangasem, Klungkung and Tabanan. The smallest administrative units are the local communities (*banjar*), which are combined to
form wards in towns and villages (*desa*) in the country; they are headed
by mayors (*walikota*).

Economy

Indonesia is one of the "emerging nations" and, until the outbreak of the
difficult financial and economic crisis, was a long-standing participant in
the economic upturn of the whole of South-East Asia. Since the beginning of 1997, when the turbulence originating in Thailand spread over
the whole region, Indonesia's further economic future is more uncertain
than ever. The annual inflation rate is about 100 per cent; 20 million
people are probably unemployed and up to 40 million live below the
poverty line. In 1997 alone the Indonesian currency lost almost two
thirds of its value.

But only a few years before, the Indonesian economy enjoyed almost
perfect economic growth. Annual increases of up to 8 per cent were the
rule and the falling value of oil exports was the only dark cloud on the
horizon of continuous, upward-pointing development. (As a member of
OPEC, the organisation of oil-producing states, Indonesia was particularly badly affected.) When asked for help, the World Bank combined its
promised aid package with the condition that the banking system – the
unrestricted credit policy of which was seen as one of the main reasons
for the crisis – be fundamentally reformed. President Habibie not only
felt himself forced to comply but he also issued an emergency regu-
lation which resulted in a drastic reduction of government expenditure
(in particular subsidies on food stuffs). This aroused greater mistrust
among the population. Habibie was accused of being ill-disposed
towards reform; not least because of his good relations with ex-
President Suharto.

The economy of Bali also suffered from the developments in the rest of Indonesia although agriculture, which is dominant on the island, was not affected to the same extent. The number of visitors also fell for a time, but since the middle of 1998 the favourable exchange rate has attracted more tourists.

Agriculture

In spite of the increasing industrialisation of Indonesia Bali has remained a predominantly agricultural province. Some 65 per cent of the island's area is under cultivation, of which around 15 per cent consists of irrigated rice-fields, 30 per cent of dry fields watered only by rain and 20 per cent of forested land, also fed only by rain.

Land use

Bali's most important crop is rice, as it has been for many centuries: the origins of the elaborate irrigation system which waters the (mostly terraced) rice-fields are believed to go back to the 6th century. Of the total Indonesian rice crop some 5 per cent is contributed by Bali, one of the country's smallest provinces. This is predominantly wet rice: that is, the young shoots are planted out by hand in fields which are kept permanently under water by damming; when the plants have reached a certain stage the water is allowed to drain away; and when the rice ripens and turns yellow it is harvested, again by hand, threshed and taken to the mills where it is husked or ground.

Rice

A feature of Balinese agricultural organisation is the grouping of the peasants in one or more village communities (*banjar*) in co-operative organisations known as *sekaha*. The *sekaha* is divided into separate sections: the *sekaha menanam* is responsible for planting, the *sekaha panem* for harvesting the crop, the *sekaha me jukut* for weeding. A fourth section, the *sekaha bajak*, does the ploughing, but is more like a neighbourly mutual aid group than a co-operative organisation. The proceeds from the sale of the agricultural produce are divided equally among the members of the sekaha after a certain amount has been set aside as a reserve.

Sekaha and subak

The co-operatives engaged in the growing of wet rice are known as subak. In southern Bali they are believed to have been established in the 16th century on the initiative of the reigning prince; in northern Bali they were started by the peasants themselves. Since at that time not all the peasants in a *banjar* had channels for the irrigation of their fields other members of the community agreed to let them have some of their water. Hence arose the obligation on every member of a *subak* not only to contribute services (e.g. the building of dams, the oversight and maintenance of the irrigation system) but also to pay a water tax.

The *subak* principle thus developed after the principle of the community of interest of the villagers, and the operation of the *subak* is still governed not by Indonesian law but by traditional customary law. Moreover it is not merely an organisation for the division of labour in the cultivation of rice: it is also a social community concerned in the religious beliefs of its members. Thus the assembly of the members of the *subak* fixes the dates of religious festivals and ceremonies in honour of the rice goddess Dewi Sri and the water god Vishnu (replaced in southern Bali by the sea god Baruna, whose particular responsibility it is to keep the rice free from pests). Each *subak* has its own temple (*pura bedugul*), situated either in the middle or on the edge of the rice-fields. The greatest festival in the rice-farmers' year is the harvest thanksgiving (*ngusaba*), when all members of the *subak* bring offerings. If any member of the subak fails to perform the tasks and obligations laid down by the community he is required to pay a fine in kind (commonly a kilogram of rice).

The *subak* is headed by a chairman elected by the assembly, who decides the distribution of the available water supply among the mem-

Threshing rice after the harvest

Tying the rice straw into sheaves

Untreated rice grains

Scarecrow

bers, settles disputes and presides over the assembly. During the Dutch colonial period a complete reorganisation of the system was planned; but while the efficiency of the irrigation system was improved the form of organisation of the *subak* remained unchanged.

Since the early eighties there have also been co-operatives organised on the model of the *sekaha* which distribute to the members loans granted by the Indonesian National Bank.

Other important Balinese crops are vegetables, rubber, tea and coffee (Bali produces over 10 per cent of the total Indonesian coffee crop). Another valuable crop is vanilla, of which Indonesia is the world's second largest supplier (after Madagascar). — Other crops

Bali's fisheries are of relatively minor importance. Round the coasts of the island there are still some 13,000 fishermen; but their earnings are so low that many fishermen's families are below the poverty line and depend on state aid. Any idea of developing the island's fisheries comes up against the Balinese belief that the sea is the abode of demons. — Fisheries

Transport

Bali has – by Asian standards – a well developed network of roads. There are no motorways, and the only stretch of road of expressway standard (with four lanes) is the Jalan Bypass round Denpasar, built to relieve congestion in the city centre. The other roads can be divided into three (non-official) categories. In the first category is the well built road circling the island, running close to the coast for part of the way – though in eastern Bali, between Singaraja and Amlapura, this road is narrower and more dangerous. There are other main roads cutting across the island from north to south. — Roads

In the second category are the roads passing through towns and villages, for the most part narrow and calling for great care in driving. The third category consists of minor roads, which are often in a lamentable state (corrugations, potholes). The verges are usually soft and there is no lighting.

There are no railways on Bali. — Railways

See Practical Information, Public Transport — Public transport

Bali is linked with an excellent network of air services. Its only airport at Ngurah Rai, a few kilometres south-west of Denpasar, is built to international standards and handles scheduled and charter flights from many countries throughout the world. — Air services

There are a variety of ferry services linking Bali with the neighbouring islands of Java and Lombok and its own offshore islands of Penida and Lembongan. The ferries carry both passengers and goods of all kinds (sometimes including livestock). There are also a number of catamaran and high-speed ferries carrying passengers only. — Shipping

Bali is a favourite port of call for cruise liners sailing in South-East Asian waters.

Tourism

Bali is the part of Indonesia best equipped to cater for tourists. Since the mid seventies a number of tourist centres with hotels of international standard have been developed, particularly in southern Bali (Nusa Dua, Kuta, Legian, Sanur).

Visitor numbers

In 1996 Indonesia still received a total of around 3.1 million visitors. Bali's share was estimated to be just under 1 million tourists from all over the world. With the outbreak of the economic crisis and its associated disturbances the number of visitors to Indonesia fell well below the 2 million mark. Only Bali, which was marginally affected by the troubles, recovered quickly and in 1998 already noted a renewed increase in visitor numbers; not least because of the favourable exchange rate for Europeans.

Visitors from the United States (about one fifth) top the tourist statistics.

History

The earliest evidence of human life in Indonesia was found on the island of Java in 1891. The remains of Java Man, belonging to the species Homo erectus (formerly called Pithecanthropus erectus), date back some 500,000 years. In the 1930s remains of early humans of Neanderthal type (Solo Man) were found on the river Solo on Java.

Prehistory

The remains of Palaeolithic cultures found on Sumatera (Sumatra), Kalimantan (Borneo) and Sulawesi (Celebes) show similarities to remains found in Indochina and Malaya, with which much of Indonesia had a land link during the Würm glaciation.

Stone Age

Archaeological evidence suggests that men of Australoid type lived on Java in the Mesolithic period. They were probably followed by Melanesoid groups, who left traces at Sampang.

During the Neolithic period Mongoloid and Veddoid groups moved into the Indonesian archipelago. They were already using simple stone implements to produce primitive textiles.

In the 2nd and 1st millennia BC there were several waves of immigration into Indonesia from the South Asian mainland.

In the 1st century BC merchants and priests come to Indonesia from Hindustan, bringing with them their religious beliefs (Buddhism, Hinduism) and establishing powerful kingdoms.

Influences from India

In the 7th century AD the Hindu kingdom of Srivijaya is established in south-eastern Sumatra, with its centre near present-day Palembang. It controls trade in the Malacca and Sunda Straits.

Kingdom of Srivijaya

Indian culture and religion influence the ruling classes of the main Indonesian islands, which by the standards of the time are densely populated. Under the Shailendra dynasty the centre of power moves to the island of Java, where in the 8th and 9th centuries magnificent structures, including the temples of Borobudur (Buddhist) and Prambanan (Hindu), are built.

Between the 13th and the 16th century the Majapahit kingdom extends its authority over extensive territories in the Indonesian archipelago. The two great Indian epics, the "Ramayana" and the "Mahabharata", recall this period.

Majapahit kingdom

From the 15th century onwards, under the influence of merchants from the Near East, Islam spreads throughout Indonesia. In the first half of the 16th century the Majapahit kingdom collapses and the sultanates of Bantam in western Java and Demak in eastern Java are founded.

Islamisation

After the discovery of the sea route to India (1487) Europeans reach Indonesia. From the early 16th century onwards the Portuguese establish forts in the eastern part of the Indonesian archipelago, not least with the idea of gaining control of the lucrative spice trade. The Spaniards and the English make little headway in this area.

Colonial rule

A hundred years later the Dutch succeed in establishing bases in Indonesia, beginning in Java. In 1602 the Dutch East India Company is founded, and under Governor-General Jan Pieterzoon Coen, founder of the town of Batavia (1619; now Jakarta), extends its influence widely throughout the region. The Dutch now have a colonial empire in South-East Asia.

History

Dutch
East Indies

During the Napoleonic wars the Dutch East Indies are occupied by Britain, and from 1811 to 1816 Stamford Raffles, the founder of Singapore, is lieutenant-governor of Java. In 1816 the territories are returned to the Netherlands, and thereafter the colonial authorities are involved in bitter fighting with rebel forces (Diponegoro rebellion, 1825–30; Aceh war, 1873–1904).

In the 1830s the colonial administration replaces the previous system of forced labour with payment in kind by a well organised plantation economy. After 1870 Indonesia is opened up to European capital and enterprise.

On August 26th–27th 1883 the volcano Krakatau (in the island group between Sumatra and Java) explodes, and tens of thousands of people in Indonesia lose their lives in an immense natural catastrophe in which some 18 cubic kilometres (4½ cubic mi.) of volcanic material are ejected, the coastal regions of south-eastern Sumatra and western Java are devastated by a tidal wave 20 m (65 ft) high, volcanic ash continues for several years to fall over an area of 800,000 sq. km (310,000 sq. mi.) and the effects are felt as far away as Australia and South America.

The discovery of oil on Sumatra in 1885 leads to the establishment of Royal Dutch Shell, which later grows into one of the world's largest oil companies.

Independence
movements

In the early years of the 20th century the colonial authorities have to contend with a number of independence movements under Islamic influence, notably Budi Utomo ("Noble Endeavour") and Sarekat Islam ("Islamic Union"). The Communist Party of Indonesia (PKI) is founded in 1920, and in 1926–27 organises a rising which is repressed without difficulty. Thereafter the movement for independence is spearheaded by the Partai Nasional Indonesia (PNI), founded in 1927 by Raden Ahmed Sukarno (see Famous People).

In the first half of the 20th century immigrants from China establish themselves in key positions in the Indonesian economy, and this subsequently leads to bitter conflicts with the Malay population.

Second World
War

During the Second World War, in 1942, the Dutch East Indies are occupied by Japanese troops, and European predominance in the region is brought to an end.

Independence

At the end of the war Indonesian nationalists organise a new state, and on August 17th 1945 unilaterally proclaim the independence of Indonesia. Sukarno becomes first President of the new Republic, with Yogyakarta and later Jakarta as its capital.

In 1947 and 1948 the Dutch try to re-establish their authority by force of arms, but under pressure from the United Nations and the United States are compelled at the Hague Conference in 1949 to recognise the independence of Indonesia (originally as the Republic of the United States of Indonesia), which until 1954 is linked with the Dutch crown in a personal union.

In mid 1959 Sukarno institutionalises his system of "guided democracy". His aim is to achieve a balance of forces (religious groups, political parties, the military) within the country. The economy is also "guided" by the state, with the object of preventing the influence of foreign companies from becoming too strong. Nevertheless the country is torn by domestic conflicts, reaching a climax in the Darul Islam rebellion.

In 1963 Indonesia gains control of Dutch New Guinea. Soon afterwards Sukarno becomes involved in a confrontation with the neighbouring country of Malaysia (in the course of which Indonesia temporarily withdraws from the United Nations, 1965–66). He increasingly co-operates with the Communists and seeks a rapprochement with the People's Republic of China.

In the autumn of 1965 the Communists launch a rising, which is crushed by General Suharto. For several months thereafter there are bloody persecutions of Communists and massacres of Chinese. In March 1966 Sukarno is overthrown by a military government headed by Suharto, which ends the policy of confrontation and seeks to resolve the country's social and economic problems with the help of the West.

In 1967 relations with the People's Republic of China are broken off, and Indonesia becomes a founder member of the Association of South-East Asian Nations (ASEAN). In 1968 Suharto has himself elected President. In 1969, in the face of international opposition, Indonesia annexes western New Guinea, which becomes the province of Irian Jaya. General elections in 1971, 1977, 1982 and 1993 produce convincing victories for the government party Sekber Golkar, a grouping of politicians with social concern, technocrats and the military. In 1976, in spite of further international protests, Indonesia annexes the Portuguese territory of Eastern Timor.

Within the grouping of "non-aligned" nations (a movement originated by the conference of African and Asian countries held at Bandung in western Java in 1950) Indonesia pursues a foreign policy which tends to lean towards the western industrial nations.

In July 1990 Indonesia resumes diplomatic relations with the People's Republic of China.

Chronology of Events on Bali

Austronesian Deutero-Malays bring Bronze and Iron Age cultures to Bali.	From 300 BC
The Hindu kingdom of Srivijaya controls much of what is now Indonesia. An irrigation system designed to improve rice crops is established on Bali.	6/7th c. AD
The Balinese prince Udaya marries the Javanese princess Mahendratta, of the Mataram dynasty. Under their son Erlangga or Airlangga (1016–42) Java and Bali are united and enjoy a cultural flowering.	9th/10th centuries
The Hindu religion gains increasing numbers of adherents on Bali.	
Kingdom of Pejeng-Bedulu on Bali.	12th century
King Kertanagara, the last ruler of the Singharasi dynasty in eastern Java, conquers Bali, but soon afterwards loses it again.	1284
Bali becomes independent.	1292
Bali is part of the powerful Majapahit kingdom, which controls much of Indonesia.	1343
Spread of Islam on Java, with persecution of non-believers. Many Hindus seek refuge on Bali.	15th/16th centuries
Collapse of the Majapahit kingdom. The son of the last king flees to Bali, where he founds the Gelgel dynasty.	c. 1520
The territory controlled by Bali reaches its greatest extent. It now includes the neighbouring island of Lombok, to the east, and the eastern tip of Java.	Early 17th century
The newly founded Dutch East India Company begins the colonisation of Indonesia.	1602
Bali splits up into a dozen independent princedoms, between which there are frequent wars.	1651

Chronology of Events on Bali

1691	The Dutch found the town of Batavia (now Jakarta) on Java.
1811–16	A brief period of British rule in the Dutch East Indies, with Stamford Raffles as lieutenant-governor of Java.
1830	The Dutch colonial authorities prescribe the crops to be grown by peasants on Bali – rubber, coffee and tea. The traditional crop, rice, is neglected, leading to periods of famine on the island.
1839	Bali under Dutch sovereignty.
1846	A Dutch expeditionary force lands on the north coast of Bali (near Singaraja) and bring part of the island under Dutch administration.
	The Dutch justification for the action is the looting of a ship which had run aground on the coast of Bali. This was a not uncommon event and was not regarded as unlawful by the Balinese, who saw any ship which struck a reef as a gift from the gods.
c. 1900	By the end of the 19th century the Dutch have established sovereignty over the whole of Indonesia.
May 1904	The looting of a ship (a Chinese sailing freighter) provides the Dutch authorities with a pretext for extending their control on Bali. The owner of the vessel accuses Balinese beachcombers of stealing the cargo, which he claims included a chest containing 2000 silver dollars.
	Without further enquiry the Dutch establish a blockade of southern Bali, bring it under colonial rule and declare war on the Raja of Badung.
September 1906	Dutch troops mount a further punitive expedition on Bali, in the course of which they also attack the civilian population. When the Dutch forces

A Balinese prince with his retinue (about 1888)

prepare to attack the palace of the Raja of Badung the Raja and his people commit ritual suicide (*puputan*). Several hundred Balinese men, women and children are massacred by the Dutch.

Bali is declared a Dutch colony.	1908

The whole of Bali is controlled by the Dutch colonial authorities.   1914

Raden Ahmed Sukarno founds the Partai Nasional Indonesia, whose aim   1927
is to liberate Indonesia from Dutch colonial rule.

The historic princedoms of Bali are restored, but never recover their   1938
former splendour and power.

During the Second World War Japanese forces occupy the whole of the   1942
Dutch East Indies, including Bali.

Unilateral proclamation of the Republic of Indonesia by Raden Ahmed   1945
Sukarno and Mohammed Hatta (August 17th).

Bali is the scene of bitter fighting during the struggle for independence   1946
(battle of Marga, August 20th). Finally the Dutch concede the island's
independence, and it becomes an autonomous region.

The Netherlands recognise the independence of the new Indonesian   1949
state, which remains linked with the Dutch crown in a personal union
until 1954.
   Bali joins the Republic of the United States of Indonesia, of which it
becomes a province (Propinsi Bali).

Only twelve years after their re-establishment the historic princedoms of   1950
Bali are again dissolved and are replaced by administrative districts.
Sukarno is elected President of the new Republic of Indonesia (August
17th).

Sukarno declares a state of emergency in the whole of Indonesia   1957
(February 21st) and announces his policy of "guided democracy".

A violent eruption of the volcano Gunung Agung claims 2500 lives   1963
(March 17th).

The Indonesian government launches a national family planning pro-   1968
gramme designed to reduce the birth rate under the slogan "Dua anak
cukup" ("Two children are enough").

The Eka Dasa Rudra ceremony, Bali's greatest Hindu festival – which had   1979
been postponed because of the eruption of Gunung Agung in May 1963
– is celebrated in the presence of President Suharto and his wife Tien.

A statistical survey puts the population of Denpasar, Bali's capital, at   1983
261,263.

A census carried out in the whole of Indonesia gives Bali a population of   1989
2.8 million. The average density of the population is around 485 to the
sq. kilometre (1256 to the sq. mile).

An earthquake on the neighbouring island of Java claims at least 120   June 1994
lives. The epicentre of the earthquake lies off the coast of Java, and
shocks are clearly felt on Bali and Lombok, but no damage is caused.

The disturbances affecting the whole of Indonesia during the economic   1997
crisis, also spread to Bali. In the capital Denpasar the shops belonging to

43

Chinese or those of Chinese descent are plundered and burnt down. However, in contrast to the other parts of Indonesia, the situation calms down after a short time. Even at the end of 1998 as the Indonesian capital Jakarta is again shaken by riots, the situation in Bali, though tense, remains quiet.

Famous People

This section contains brief biographies, in alphabetical order, of notable people connected with Bali or Indonesia.

The writer Vicki Baum, born in Vienna, spent nine months on Bali at a time when the Dutch authorities, after years of conflict, had brought the island almost completely under their control. Fascinated by the people of Bali, who preserved their own culture in spite of their foreign masters, she wrote a novel, "A Tale from Bali" (1937), which shows a profound understanding of the history of the island and its people and the mentality of the Balinese. In her picture of life in a Balinese village she shows the influence – the very superficial influence – of the Dutch colonial rulers on the traditional life of the villagers.
Vicki Baum died in Hollywood in 1960.

Vicki Baum
Austrian writer
(1888–1960)

The Spanish painter Antonio María Blanco occupies a leading place among the artists who have chosen to work on Bali. After attending school in Manila (Philippines) he studied at the Academy of Art in New York and thereafter lived successively in Florida, California, Honolulu and Japan. In 1952 he visited Bali for the first time. Impressed by his work, which had won numerous prizes, the son of the Raja of Ubud gave him a former summer palace, set in beautiful gardens, as a house and studio. After leaving Bali for some years he returned there, married a Balinese wife and settled permanently on the island. Some years ago he converted most of his house in Ubud into a museum.

Antonio María
Blanco
Spanish painter
(b. 1926)

Blanco's work combines humorous and impressionistic features with erotic elements. He is a master of the self-portrait.

The Spanish painter Antonio Blanco

Famous People

Vicki Baum

Walter Spies

Raden Ahmed Sukarno

Walter Spies
German painter
and musician
(1895–1942)

Born in Moscow, the son of a wealthy and respected merchant family, Walter Spies became a painter, whose work was strongly influenced by his stay on Bali. He lived in Moscow until the age of 15 and then went to Dresden, where he attended the Gymnasium (grammar school). He spent the First World War in a Russian internment camp in the Urals, where he acquired his love of nature.

After his release he returned to Dresden and then lived for a time in Berlin, where he became friendly with painters such as the Expressionists Oskar Kokoschka and Otto Dix, one of the most famous representatives of the Neue Sachlichkeit movement, and with the composer Ernst Krenek. In September 1923 he left Germany and sailed in a freighter from Hamburg to Java, where during the first few weeks after his arrival he earned his keep by playing the piano in bars. In January 1924 the Sultan of Yogyakarta appointed him conductor of the western-style court orchestra which he had formed.

Thereafter he gained a considerable reputation as a musicologist. He learned to play all the instruments in the gamelan orchestra and became a keen collector of old Javanese (and later Balinese) music, which he introduced to the western world on instruments tuned to western keys. In April 1925 Spies visited Bali for the first time, and two years later settled permanently on the island. Fascinated by the scenery and the people of Bali, he lived at first in the palace of the art-loving Raja of Ubud, and later built his own house, which became the meeting-place of numerous artists who lived on Bali or visited the island; among them was Vicki Baum (see entry), who wrote her novel "A Tale from Bali" while staying in his house. Spies influenced local Balinese painters, but also learned much from them, particularly from their mental attitude to art.

When German troops invaded the Netherlands in May 1940 Spies was interned with other German nationals in the Dutch East Indies. In January 1942, only a few days before the Japanese invasion, the ship in which the internees were being transferred to India was sunk by a Japanese flying bomb; there were only a few survivors, and Spies was not among them.

Walter Spies is still much admired on Bali. Some of his finest works can be seen in the Neka Museum in Ubud.

Raden Ahmed
Sukarno
Indonesian
politician
(1901–70)

Raden Ahmed Sukarno, founder of the sovereign state of Indonesia, was born in Bitar (Java), the son of a Javanese father and a Balinese mother. After attending school in Surabaya and taking a degree in engineering he turned at the age of 26 to politics and in 1927 founded the Partai

Nasional Indonesia (PNI), whose object was to secure independence for Indonesia. Arrested by the Dutch colonial authorities, he spent the years 1929–32 in prison; then in 1933 he was exiled to the island of Flores and in 1938 to Sumatra. After being released by the Japanese in 1942 he collaborated with them in the hope of gaining independence for his country.

Sukarno's declared aim was to shake off the yoke of colonial rule. His greatest difficulty was to persuade all the Balinese princes that common action was necessary to found a unified state. He finally achieved this on August 17th 1945, when together with Mohammed Hatta, a companion in arms in the underground movement which fought the Dutch forces, he proclaimed the independence of Indonesia – though this was not recognised by the Dutch until 1949. There were, however, differences between the two men: Sukarno sought to establish a "guided democracy" headed by a strong man, while Hatta preferred a democracy on the western model.

Sukarno was constantly concerned to achieve a balance between the various political and social groupings in Indonesia. The basis for this was provided by the Five Principles (Panca Sila), in which he sought to combine Javanese/Hindu, Islamic and socialist values.

During Sukarno's period of rule the Communist parties in many Asian countries became increasingly influential. Towards the end of the 1950s he drew closer to the People's Republic of China and from 1963 onwards distanced himself from Malaysia. It was not clear how far he was involved in the attempted *coup d'état* instigated by the Communists in 1965, and this was one of the reasons for his fall from power two years later. First his powers as President were reduced and then, in 1967, General Suharto deposed him and put him under house arrest for the rest of his life.

Sukarno died in Jakarta on June 21st 1970.

Culture

The Balinese occupy a special position among the peoples of Indonesia, largely because in spite of attacks and intrusions from outside the island they have managed to preserve their religious traditions and thus also their cultural independence. This does not mean that over the centuries Bali has remained completely uninfluenced by other cultures and in consequence isolated from the rest of the Indonesian world; but the central element in Balinese life has always remained Hinduism – even though, as now practised on Bali, it tends towards monotheism in the worship of the god Sangyang Widi. Against this background there were, of course, changes in cultural life, and these inevitably affected Balinese art.

Compared with the variety of artistic techniques found, for example, on the neighbouring island of Java before its Islamisation, Balinese art, particularly in the earlier centuries, may appear to be of the nature of folk art, producing work of modest quality. Against this it can be claimed that Balinese temples, for example, gain from the simplicity of their form and decoration. In looking at any Balinese work of art we should bear in mind that the artist's hand is always guided by religion. The representation of religious themes and motifs, whether in flat or in plastic form, is always merely a means to an end: its sole purpose is to make religion and religious ideas understandable to the beholder.

For a glossary of mythological, religious and artistic terms, see pp. 61–64.

Temples

Compared with the lavish and colourful splendour of the temples of Thailand, Balinese temples are sober, functional buildings. On the occasion of a festival a Balinese temple is magnificently decked with flowers and brightly coloured ribbons and fabrics; but a temple in which no festival is being celebrated or is about to be celebrated stands empty and abandoned; often it will be locked.

The island of Bali itself is sometimes seen as one large temple, in which the western tip of the island, with the port of Gilimanuk, is the entrance and the hills at the east end (Gunung Agung and Gunung Batur) are symbols of Meru, the sacred mountain. Most of the temples of Bali are oriented on these hills (*kaja*, "towards the mountain"), with the entrance facing towards the sea (*kelod*, "towards the sea").

There are over 20,000 temples (*pura*) on Bali, not counting the family temples (*sanggah*) in every *pekarangan* or *kampong* (family compound). The highest rank is occupied by the "royal temples", of which (according to an unofficial count) there are six, the most important being the Pura Besakih, the "temple of all temples".

Other much revered temples are the sea temple Pura Tanah Lot and the mountain temple Pura Batukau. They are maintained by the state or the old princely families, which still remain influential.

Also much revered are a number of temples dedicated to the gods of the mountains, seas, rivers and springs. There are also temples equipped with bathing-places both for gods and for men (e.g. the Pura Tirtha Empul at Ubud).

In general a village community has not merely one temple, but three. The *pura puseh* is the principal temple, dedicated to Brahma, the god of

◀ *Bale (pavilion) and kori agung (covered gate)*

Candi bentar (split gate)

creation; it is always situated on the side of the village facing the sacred mountain Gunung Agung. In the *pura desa* (also called the *pura bale agung*), which is dedicated to Vishnu, preserver of the order of the world, the village community meets to perform the all-important religious ceremonies. The *pura dalem*, usually situated outside the village near the place of cremation and dedicated to Durga (the goddess of death and destruction, an incarnation of Shiva), is used for the ceremonies associated with a cremation; it is always oriented towards the sea.

The Balinese temples are not intended to serve all the inhabitants of the island: they belong either to a family, the village community as a whole, a particular professional group or a caste. The state or "royal" temples mentioned above are an exception to this: they are used by all the inhabitants of the island in common.

Layout

The layout of a Balinese temple is similar to that of a family compound. It is always oriented towards the mountain and usually consists of three courtyards, which symbolise not only the three worlds (the upper, middle and lower worlds) but also the eternal cycle of birth, death and rebirth.

The first courtyard (*jaba sisi*), which usually contains only secular buildings, leads into the middle courtyard (*jaba tengah*), in which the worshippers gather during a temple festival in order to prepare, and to prepare themselves, for the arrival of the gods. Beyond this is the *jeroan*, the most sacred precinct of the temple, which is exclusively reserved for

Raksasa, a terrifying demon

Vishnu mounted on Garuda

the gods and their earthly representatives, the priests. Ordinary people may enter it only to bring offerings.

Elements

The entrance to the first courtyard of a temple is almost always through a *candi bentar* (split gate), with a fairly narrow opening. The form of the gate is explained by a legend: it is said that when Mount Meru, the abode of all the Hindu gods, was being transported to Bali it broke into two parts, which then formed the two mountains Gunung Agung and Gunung Batur. The *candi bentar* symbolises the two broken halves of Mount Meru; it is usually richly decorated.

Candi bentar

The *candi korung* (covered gate) or *kori agung* leads from the second courtyard into the third part of the temple. It is elaborately decorated and richly ornamented; for the innermost courtyard of the temple symbolises Mount Meru and thus, to the Hindus, the highest of all worlds.

Candi korung

Beyond the covered gate is the *aling-aling*, a protective wall designed to keep out evil spirits and demons, which can only move straight ahead and cannot turn right to get round the wall. They may not even get so far, since on either side of the gate are two particularly hideous demons (*raksasa*), designed so to terrify their fellow-demons that they will not venture to enter the sacred precinct.

Aling-aling

A *bale*, of which there may be several within the precincts of a temple, is an open-sided pavilion. In a *pura desa* (one of the three temples in a Balinese village the *bale* is known as the *bale agung* and serves as the meeting-place of the village elders. In a large temple with several *bales*

Bale

51

they may be used, for example, in the preparation of offerings for a temple festival.

Gedong

A *gedong* is a shrine, which may be small (*gedong penimpanan*) or large (*gedong agung*). A *gedong penimpanan* contains all that is required for the accommodation of gods and divinities during their stay on earth. This may include a small statue, an elaborately carved mask or a kris (dagger). A *gedong agung* is a shrine for the veneration of ancestors.

Padmasana

The arrangement of the seating for the gods varies from place to place. In southern Bali the richly decorated stone throne (*padmasana*) is in the north-east corner of the sacred precinct, while in northern Bali it stands in the centre. This is because the back of the throne must always face in the direction of the sacred mountain, Gunung Agung. The throne is in three parts: the lowest part symbolises the lower world, the middle part the middle world and the uppermost part Mount Meru. The highest throne in the sacred precinct belongs to the god Shiva, who is known on Bali as Sangyang Widi and visits the earth under that name. Where other seats are provided they are intended for other divinities of varying rank.

These seats are not symbols of the gods and divinities concerned but their actual property.

Meru

The *meru* is a pagoda-like structure in the innermost precinct of a temple which symbolises Mount Meru, the abode of all the Hindu divinities. It has a number of tiered roofs (*tumpang*) covered with palm-leaves, rice straw or merely corrugated iron.

Pelinggih

The god permanently resident in a temple lives in the *pelinggih*, a shrine with either one or two roofs, leaving it only once a year, on the occasion

A temple decorated for the odalan *festival*

of the *odalan* festival (see p. 30). Above the main roofs are up to eleven tiered roofs, again symbolising Mount Meru.

In addition to the main buildings within the temple precinct there may be varying numbers of other pavilions, shrines, altars for offerings and pagodas.

The bell-tower (*kulkul*) is usually in the first courtyard of a temple. The "bell", which is used to summon worshippers to prayer or to meetings and festivals in the temple or as an alarm, is usually made from a hollowed tree trunk (more rarely of metal). It is struck in time by two men or boys, with varying rhythms for different purposes.

Kulkul

Sculpture

It is not certain whether there was any real sculpture on Bali in the pre-Hindu period (i.e. up to the end of the 1st millennium A.D.). The general opinion of scholars is that the early Balinese places of worship were usually undecorated. A fresh stimulus was given to Balinese art by Hinduism with its variety of artistic techniques. More recently, however, archaeological finds have shown that the Balinese were well able to produce plastic representations, predominantly in the form of reliefs, of venerated figures of the Buddhist and later the Hindu religion. It is very probable that Javanese influence played a part in this. With the increasing influence of Hinduism on Balinese art, at any rate by the time when persecuted Javanese Hindus, undoubtedly including priests and artists, sought refuge on Bali (15th–16th c.), Balinese art was strongly and unmistakably influenced by Javanese features.

Thereafter the representation of divinities (see Hindu Pantheon, p. 23) featured prominently in Balinese art. In the field of plastic art the earlier bas-reliefs and high reliefs were now supplemented by sculpture in the round on the Indian model. Works of this period are excavated from time to time, and some are to be seen in temples on Bali. In the subsequent development of reliefs the Balinese delight in a luxuriant proliferation of ornament is very evident. The constant repetition of detail, without losing its effect on the beholder, is the characteristic that marks out the distinctively Balinese relief from the Javanese style.

Changes are also noticeable in architecture. Whereas until the period of transition to Hinduism the tufa walls round a temple, for example, were plain and undecorated, they were now ornamented with sculpture on the front and at the corners – mainly grimacing figures of demons and witches intended to frighten off their fellow-demons and keep them out of the sacred precinct. Elsewhere we find themes from the "Ramayana" and the "Mahabharata" (see pp. 59–60) or scenes of everyday life on Bali.

Modern sculpture continues to follow the model of earlier centuries. Any further development is inhibited, if only because of the need to replace older statues and sculpture destroyed by the ravages of time.

Painting

Balinese painting, which has retained throughout its history features of simple folk art, has developed over the centuries in a consistent way. Few examples of early painting have survived, since the artists painted mainly on textiles which do not keep well. They depicted scenes which also occurred in the Balinese shadow plays (*wayang kulit*: see p. 58). Early Balinese painting thus sought to "freeze" fleeting moments of

Kulkul (bell-tower)

Balinese painting

action. The pigments used (predominantly warm tones like red, orange, ochre, yellow and a clear white) were of purely organic origin. One of the finest examples of early Balinese painting is to be seen in the Kerta Gosa (Court Hall) in Klungkung.

European influences

When numbers of artists painting in the western manner began to come to Bali this led to marked changes in the style, form of expression and content of Balinese painting. One of the most important innovations introduced by such western artists as Walter Spies (see Famous People), Le Mayeur, Rudolf Bonnet and W. O. J. Nieuwenkamp was that Balinese painting, which had hitherto been two-dimensional, now acquired a third dimension. At the same time there was a change in the content of the picture: whereas in the past the foreground and background had scarcely been distinguished from one another the scene now centred on the figures who formed the subject of the picture.

The European painters founded painting schools in which they taught young Balinese artists European painting techniques but were cautious about influencing their form of expression or style. Modern Balinese painting, therefore, has lost little of its inherited expressiveness and originality.

Woodcarving

Like other arts, Balinese woodcarving has a religious and cultural significance, even though the prime function of many objects (e.g. jars and dishes) is a practical, everyday one. Particularly famous are the elaborately carved wooden masks, of which there are two types: those which

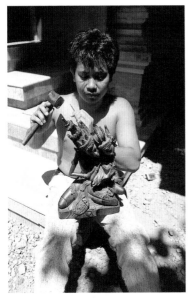

Woodcarvers ...   *... at work*

are of high religious value and accordingly do not come on to the market and those which are made for the souvenir trade. The uninstructed visitor will not notice the difference, since both types of mask have the same names (e.g. Rangda masks). There are also a great variety of dancers' masks (e.g. the Barong mask) worn in performances of traditional Balinese dances.

The production of a Rangda mask, as worn in religious festivals, particularly in dances, is subject to a variety of prescriptions. It must be made exclusively from the wood of the *pohon pule* tree, and the trunk must be brought in from the forest at a time determined by a priest on the basis of complicated calculations. When the mask has been completed and painted (exclusively with organic paints) it is said that holy water (*tirtha*) flows from it every 32 days.

Many other beautiful objects are produced by Balinese woodcarvers. Whole families live by the creation of wooden figures in a timeless modern style. Since the 1920s there has been a fashion for producing figures of exaggerated slenderness. Fine woodcarving is not cheap, for the Balinese mentality insists on the exclusive use of the time-consuming method of production by hand.

Textiles

Although the origins of batik are probably to be looked for on Java (where the finest batik is still produced), the Balinese have developed an extraordinary skill in the art. In the main tourist centres there are now schools which run special courses in batik work.

Batik

Dance

Ikat

Ikat is a special process which developed out of batik but is very different from it. In this complex technique the colours are dyed into the thread (either the warp or the weft) before weaving, those areas which are to remain uncoloured being bound tightly together: hence the name *ikat*, which means to bind or to knot. A distinction is made between warp ikats (in which the warp, the threads stretched vertically on the loom, is dyed) and weft ikats (in which the horizontal threads fed through the warp by the shuttle are dyed).

Double ikat

Double ikat is a still more complex process practised only in the Balinese village of Tenganan and on the neighbouring island of Lombok. In this technique both the warp and the weft threads are dyed. The production of a piece of cloth in the double ikat technique may take months or even years. Double ikat fabrics are credited with magical powers.

Dance

Balinese dances play an important part in both secular and religious life, and the many forms of dance can be seen as a means of giving living expression to religion. No temple festival is celebrated without several performances of dances. Since, however, such events usually take place when the visitors are back in their hotels special performances, in more easily understandable form, are now put on for their benefit; information about them can be obtained from travel agencies in the tourist centres.

Baris

The *baris* is danced exclusively by men, armed with a variety of weapons. Out of the original form, in which no dancer had a leading role, there developed in course of time a form which lays emphasis on the skill of an individual solo dancer. The *baris* gives expression to all the various emotions and feelings of a warrior – courage and fear, compassion and ruthlessness in face of the enemy, joy over victory and sorrow over defeat. The accompaniment by the gamelan orchestra follows the movements of the dancer, not the other way round.

Barong

The Barong is the most famous of the Balinese dances and the most frequently performed. There are several versions, though the differences between them are minor. The Barong tells a complicated story, and can be seen as a drama in several acts rather than merely a dance. To the accompaniment of a gamelan orchestra the dancers, wearing animal masks, come on to the stage one by one, and the performance begins with a solo *legong* dance (see below). The principal characters are the witch Rangda, who wears a terrifying hand-carved mask, and the Barong, a lion-like figure operated by two dancers. Rangda symbolises evil, while the Barong stands for good; but which of them is victorious remains open.

Kebyar

The *kebyar*, which developed in its present form about 1915, is of all the solo dances of Bali perhaps the one most laden with symbolism. Although it is danced by a grown man its theme is the moods and temptations of a pubescent boy. The interest of this dance lies not in the costume (which as a rule consists only of a cloth with a long tail wound round the hips) but in the miming and gestures of the dancer, who sits cross-legged on the ground and "dances" only with his torso and his arms and hands. The *kebyar* was brought to its highest perfection by the famous performer known as Mario.

Kecak

The *kecak*, which is danced only by men, is one of the most memorable of the ritual dances which visitors to Bali will experience; it is cer-

The Barong dance

Balinese dances are of many kinds

tainly the noisiest. It is also the youngest of the Balinese dances, being created in its present form only in the 1930s, when elements from the Indian epic, the "Ramayana", were introduced into the story of the dance. The idea came from the German painter Walter Spies (see Famous People) before the shooting of the film "Bali, Island of Demons". Originally the *kecak* was performed to drive out evil spirits and demons. In this dance a large group of men, between 70 and 100 in number, with bare torsos sit in a circle, symbolising the followers of the monkey Hanuman. The *kecak* takes its name from the loud chanting of the men ("chak-chak"), accompanied by movements of their arms and bodies.

Legong

If the *kebyar* has as its theme the moods of a pubescent boy the *legong* can be seen as its female counterpart – though it is concerned with the onset of puberty only in so far as a girl's first menstruation disqualifies her from dancing the *legong*. A flawless body and, of course, virginity were the essential requirements before a girl was allowed, at the age of around five, to begin to learn the *legong*. As in many Asian dances, the "language of the hands and fingers" plays an important part in the *legong*. Every movement of the body, every position of the hands and every movement of the fingers has its significance. The *legong* is danced by three girls, one of whom begins alone, telling the story of Raja Lasem, a prince's son who seeks the favour of the maiden Rangkesari, is rejected by her and finally dies in battle. During the dance the girls change their roles but not their costumes – so that, though visitors will be impressed by the beauty of the dance, they may find it difficult to follow the story.

Kris

The most important element in this dance is the kris, the Indonesian dagger with a scalloped edge which is believed to possess magical powers and to be inhabited by a protective spirit. Always hand-made and usually elaborately ornamented, the kris is the pride of every Balinese man, the symbol of his full membership of the village community. The craftsmen who specialise in making krisses are among the most highly regarded professional groups on Bali, and the method of making a kris is passed on by word of mouth from generation to generation. But even the most respected kris-maker cannot go to work until a Brahman has been asked to determine the most favourable time for forging the metal.

Music

Gamelan

No Balinese village is without a gamelan orchestra, and many of them have several. Gamelan is a general term which covers a number of different groups of musicians, which may be quite small (*gamelan legong*) or may include anything up to 30 or 40 players (*gamelan gong*). The gamelan orchestra plays a part in all kinds of festivals on Bali as well as in dances, drama and the shadow play.

History

The origins of Balinese music are to be sought on the neighbouring island of Java, though in the course of centuries different combinations of instruments and different names for the instruments developed on Bali. The name gamelan (meaning "grasp") itself comes from Java. It seems certain that at the time, during the first millennium B.C., when men in Asia learned how to make bronze the first instruments in that metal were also produced. Whether instruments were also made, either earlier or later, from other materials such as wood is unknown.

Scales

In contrast to the octave of western music, based on a system of seven intervals with semitones and whole tones which are in turn divided into twelve semitone steps, Balinese music usually has an octave of five notes (Javanese *slendro*). There are three scales, each of five full notes, and the notes in these pentatonic scales are separated from one another by approximately the same intervals; there are no semitones. In addition there are scales of seven, six or four notes, which are used according to the particular occasion on which the gamelan orchestra is playing: thus the group playing at a funeral ceremony (*anklung*) uses a scale of only four notes.

Balinese music also differs in metre from western music. As a rule the time is duple (two beats to the bar), differentiated only by varying tempos.

A feature common to all gamelan orchestras is that the players are not confined to one instrument but may play several; thus in the *gamelan gong* a group of 30 to 40 players will play up to 80 instruments between them. There is a wide range of instruments. Among instruments providing the melody are the *gender panembung* (bronze plates suspended over pipes tuned to particular keys), gongs tuned to high, middle and low notes, *bonangs* (small metal vessels suspended from a wooden frame), bamboo flutes and the *rebab* (a stringed instrument with a curving soundbox).

The rhythm is supplied by drums (*gendang*) of varying size and tone. A variation from the sequence of notes played by the instruments supplying the melody is provided by the *gender barung* (similar to the *gender panembung* but with more octaves) and the *tilempang*), a kind of zither.

There are many other instruments which may be included in the gamelan orchestra according to requirements – all made of the same materials as those already mentioned. The instruments are all made by hand in accordance with numerous rules which have been laid down by

A gamelan orchestra

tradition and must be strictly observed. Old instruments are particularly admired; some of them, indeed, are regarded as sacred and may be played only by a few selected musicians and only in important ceremonies and festivals.

Present situation

Balinese music was handed down from generation to generation over many centuries without being written down, and even today it is still a common practice – though now in accordance with strict formal rules – to improvise or play from memory.

In earlier times a few basic tunes were noted down on palm leaves, but it was only thanks to the work of the German-born painter and musician Walter Spies (see Famous People) and the American musicologist Colin McPhee (1900–64), who studied Balinese music in the 1920s and 1930s, that a number of pieces of music for gamelan orchestras were recorded in a notation devised for the purpose and thus became available to a western public.

Wayang

Shadow theatre

Although the shadow theatre (*Wayang Kulit*) is found all over Asia it has developed a distinctive form on Bali. In the performance of a shadow play, which may last several hours, the operator (*dalang*) stands behind a white screen lit by a flickering oil lamp. It is his task to give life to the characters in the play, which are flat figures usually made of tanned buf-

Balinese shadow play figures

falo skin; and this he does with extraordinary skill, manipulating anything up to ten figures at the same time.

The plot of the play is based on themes from the two great Indian epics, the "Ramayana" and the "Mahabharata" (see below, Literature). A shadow play is a regular item in any temple festival, and is sometimes also performed during the ceremonies associated with a rite of passage. The audience, of all ages, sit in front of the screen, following with fascination and sometimes with breathless excitement the movements of the characters and the script, which is usually in the form of a monologue. The play is accompanied by a small gamelan orchestra.

Masked theatre

In the masked theatre (*Wayang Topeng*), as the name implies, the mask is of more importance than the person who wears it. When the dancer takes the mask out of the cloth in which it is wrapped and puts it on he also takes on the character indicated by the mask. Before actually putting it on, therefore, he is allowed a period of meditation so that he may think himself into the part. *Topeng* masks can be bought in souvenir shops, but such masks could never be worn in a *wayang topeng*. True *topeng* masks are regarded as possessing a soul of their own and as sacred, and accordingly they must be made in accordance with prescribed rituals. The plot of a masked play consists of stories of the time when Bali was ruled by princes.

Literature

The origins of Balinese literature are to be found in Indian writings. Hindu missionaries brought to Bali, as to many other Asian countries, stories, tales, fairytales and legends from India, which were altered by the Balinese in accordance with their own ideas. In most cases, however, the original source can still be detected.

The most important story of Indian origin is the "Ramayana", a kind of knightly epic poem whose central theme is the perpetual conflict between gods and demons. The first parts of this work, which had a total of 24,000 four-line verses, may have been composed as early as the 3rd century B.C. Later two anonymous chroniclers added two further books, in which the hero of the story becomes an incarnation of the god Vishnu. The "Ramayana", however, admits of more than one interpretation, and – depending on varying religious views – there are regional variations, which frequently include only part of the original plot. The following account is based on the version current on Bali.

Vishnu comes down to earth for the seventh time in the person of Rama and is born as one of the three sons of Raja Desarata, king of Ayodhya (a town on the river Sarayu in northern India). Rama falls in love with the king's daughter Sita (also called Sinta), and wins her father's favour as the only man able to draw his bow.

The problem now arises that many years ago Raja Desarata had promised his first wife to fulfil her two wishes. Although he would like to make Rama, his favourite son, his successor, he is compelled to bend to the will of his former wife and declare his second son, Betara, heir to the throne.

Still harder is the second demand that he should banish Rama from his kingdom for fifteen years. When Desarata dies and Betara succeeds to the throne Rama and Sita leave their home town, although Betara offers to renounce the throne in favour of his half-brother.

The fair Sita is then carried off by the demon king Rawana, who seeks to compel her to live with him. Rama now recalls the task assigned to

Ramayana

him by Brahma of destroying the demon king. Brahma had once assured Rawana that no god could defeat him; and as a means of getting round this assurance he bethought himself of the ruse of sending Vishnu down to earth reborn as a man.

After a number of adventures Rama succeeds in defeating Rawana with the help of the monkey king Sukriwa and the monkey Hanuman. Hanuman manages to find his way into Sita's prison and tell her that Rama is coming to free her. He is captured by Rawana but contrives to escape and to set fire to the palace with his burning tail.

With the help of the sea god Waruna one of the monkeys builds a bridge from India to the island of Ceylon (Sri Lanka), enabling Rama and his retinue to escape. Rawana pursues him and involves him in a bloody conflict lasting six days and six nights, from which Rama finally emerges victorious.

Rama and Sita now return to their home town, where Betara again offers to give up the throne. The people of the town are against this unless Sita can show that Rawana has not influenced her with his evil thoughts. She withstands the test, demonstrating her innocence by emerging unscathed from a burning pyre.

Mahabharata | Still longer than the "Ramayana" is the "Mahabharata", which consists of 110,000 double lines. The story is thought to have a historical basis, the conflict between the Pandava (the five sons of Pandu) and the Kaurava (the 49 sons of the blind Raja Desarata) for possession of the territory of present-day Delhi.

Here too the main story is overlaid with a variety of other poems, legends of gods and heroes, love stories and religious and philosophical dissertations which are only loosely connected with the central action.

The "Mahabharata" was composed between the 4th century B.C. and the 4th century A.D. The most important part of the poem from the point of view of Hinduism is the section relating events before the decisive battle between the Pandava and the Kaurava.

Glossary

Terms in mythology, religion and art

This Glossary is designed to help the visitor to Bali who may have difficulty with the unfamiliar technical terms used in the fields of mythology, religion and art. Of the very numerous terms in use only a selection can be given here.

Adat Traditional customary law.

Aling-aling A low protective wall behind the covered gate (see Candi korung) of a temple, designed to keep out demons and evil spirits.

Bade The sarcophagus in which the body of a dead person is carried to the place of cremation.

Bale A pavilion-like building within a family compound or a temple. It is usually open on all sides, with the roof supported on pillars. In a temple there are normally several bales.

Bale agung A pavilion where elders or married men of a village meet.

Bali aga Old Balinese.

Bale banjar A pavilion in which the members of a banjar meet.

Bale gong A large pavilion in the middle one of the (usually) three court-yards of a temple, in which the gamelan orchestra (see entry) plays during a temple festival and the musical instruments are kept.

Bale pesamyangan A pavilion within a temple in which the gods are received at the beginning of a temple festival. Since the worshippers never know how many gods will be coming it is usually a large building.

Bale pesimpangan A pavilion for the accommodation of the gods who do not live permanently in the temple but merely come on a visit.

Bale piasan A pavilion in which offerings are displayed or prepared.

Banjar Part of a village community (see Desa). The members of a banjar are the married men of that part of the village.
At the regular meetings of a banjar all matters of importance concerning it, including disputes between members, are discussed and decided. Decisions reached by the banjar (normally by a majority) are binding on all members.

Barong A fabulous animal of Hindu mythology. In contrast to the witch Rangda (see entry) the Barong has a healing power.

Bayu Indian deity (God of Wind).

A bale in the princely palace, Denpasar

Bedawang A turtle as a symbol of the underworld; one of the ten incarnations of the god Vishnu. It has one or two snakes coiling round it, and always forms the base of a lotus throne (see Padmasana).

Candi Gate.

Candi bentar The "split gate" of a temple. Its curious form is explained by the legend that when Mount Meru, the abode of the gods, was being transported to Bali it broke into two parts, which then formed the two mountains of Gunung Agung and Gunung Batur. The split gate symbolises these two sacred Balinese mountains. Tapering towards the top, it resembles a mountain which has been split through the middle and divided into two equal parts.

Candi korung The covered gate of a temple, normally the entrance to the innermost precinct and usually richly decorated. On either side of the gate (also called kori agung) there are frequently guardian witches or demons (see Raksasa) whose function is to frighten off the evil spirits of the underworld and keep them out of the most sacred part of the temple. The covered gate also symbolises the three "passages" in a Hindu's life – birth, death and rebirth.

Desa A village community, consisting of a number of banjars.

Dewi danu Tutelary Goddess of Water.

Dewi sri Tutelary Goddess of Rice Plants

Gamelan An orchestra of varying size, mostly playing on gongs and other percussion instruments; sometimes also stringed instruments.

The monkey god of Hanuman   *Mask of the witch Rangda*

Gedong adung A building in which ancestors are venerated.

Gedong Penimpanan Small buildings containing items which provide shelter for deities visiting Earth.

Indra Indian God of Wind.

Jaba First courtyard of a temple.

Jaba tengah Second courtyard of a temple.

Jeroam Third and innermost courtyard of a temple.

Kori agung See Candi korung.

Kris An Indonesian dagger credited with magical qualities (see p. 58).

Kilkul Bell-tower. The "bell" is usually a hollowed tree-trunk. It not only summons worshippers to a temple festival or an important meeting but also serves as an alarm in the event of fire or other danger.

Linga(m) A phallic symbol of stone or wood. The word comes from Sanskrit and means "sign". The lingam symbolises the god Shiva and his creative potency.

"Mahabharata" An Indian epic in 110,000 double lines relating the story of the conflict of the Pandava and the Kaurava for possession of the territory of present-day Delhi.

Padmasana The lotus throne on which the god Shiva sits in his manifestation as the sun god Surya. The back of a padmasana always faces in the direction of Gunung Agung, and its base is the turtle of the underworld, Bedawang (see entry).

Padur raksa Special form of Candi Korung.

Pelinggih The shrine for a divinity who lives permanently in the temple. For gods who come only on a visit there is the bale pesimpangan.

Prasada A special form of gate resembling a pagoda which symbolises the veneration of the ancestors of a princely family.

Pura Temple (Sanskrit).

Pura dalem/desa/puseh The three temples of a village community. The pura dalem is dedicated to Shiva, the pura desa to Vishnu, the pura puseh to the creator god Brahma. The most important of the three is the pura desa, the "temple of life". In the pura dalem, the temple of the underworld (sometimes also the temple of the ancestors) the ceremonies associated with cremation are celebrated.

Pura subak A small temple, to which the members of a subak (see entry) bring offerings.

Puri The palace of a noble family.

Raksasa The figure or mask of a demon or witch.

"Ramayana" An Indian epic ("Ramayana" = "In Praise of Rama"), which may have originated in the 3rd century BC, telling in 24,000 four-line verses the story of Rama (an incarnation of Shiva) and his wife Sita.

Rangda A witch who incarnates the principle of destruction; one of the manifestations of Shiva, destroyer of the worlds.

Sangyang basuki Serpent of the underworld.

Sangyang Widi The supreme divine principle, reflecting the trend in Balinese Hinduism towards monotheism, the belief in a single god who carries within himself the qualities of all the gods of Hinduism.

Sawah An irrigated rice-field, usually terraced.

Subak A co-operative organisation of rice-farmers whose fields are irrigated by the same main channel. It is the responsibility of the subak to organise work in the rice-fields and to maintain the irrigation system. The profits of the subak are divided equally among the members, after setting aside a reserve against bad times.

Trimurti The divine trinity of Brahma, Vishnu and Shiva.

Tumpang A tier in the upper part of a pagoda; a roof.

Wada The sarcophagus in which the body of a member of the Jaba (rice-farmers') caste is carried to the place of cremation, corresponding to the bade (see entry) in other castes.

Waringin tree A sacred tree (usually within a temple).

Wayang Play; theatre.

Wayang kulit Shadow play (see p. 60).

Wayang topeng Masked play (see p. 61).

Quotations

It was on the 13th of June, 1856, after a twenty days' passage from Singapore in the "Kembang Djepoon" ("Rose of Japan"), a schooner belonging to a Chinese merchant, manned by a Javanese crew, and commanded by an English captain, that we cast anchor in the dangerous roadstead of Bileling on the north side of the island of Bali. Going on shore with the captain and the Chinese supercargo, I was at once introduced to a novel and interesting scene. We went first to the house of the Chinese Bandar, or chief merchant, where we found a number of natives, well-dressed, and all conspicuously armed with krisses, displaying their large handles of ivory or gold, or beautifully grained and polished wood.

Alfred Russel Wallace British zoologist (1823–1913)

The Chinamen had given up their national costume and adopted the Malay dress, and could then hardly be distinguished from the natives of the island – an indication of the close affinity of the Malayan and Mongolian races. Under the thick shade of some mango-trees close by the house, several women-merchants were selling cotton goods; for here the women trade and work for the benefit of their husbands, a custom which Mahometan Malays never adopt ... We then took a walk to look at the village. It was a very dull and dreary place; a collection of narrow lanes bounded by high mud walls, enclosing bamboo houses, into some of which we entered and were very kindly received ...

A slightly undulating plain extends from the sea-coast about ten or twelve miles inland, where it is bounded by a fine range of wooded and cultivated hills. Houses and villages, marked out by dense clumps of cocoa-nut palms, tamarind and other fruit trees, are dotted about in every direction; while between them extend luxuriant rice-grounds, watered by an elaborate system of irrigation that would be the pride of the best cultivated parts of Europe. The whole surface of the country is divided into irregular patches, from many acres to a few perches in extent, each of which is itself perfectly level, but stands a few inches or several feet above or below those adjacent to it. Every one of these patches can be flooded or drained at will, by means of a system of ditches and small channels, into which are diverted the whole of the streams that descend from the mountains. Every patch now bore crops in various stages of growth, some almost ready for cutting, and all in the most flourishing condition and of the most exquisite green tints.

The sides of the lanes and bridle roads were often edged with prickly Cacti and a leafless Euphorbia, but the country being so highly cultivated there was not much room for indigenous vegetation, except upon the sea- beach. We saw plenty of the fine race of domestic cattle descended from the Bos banteng of Java, driven by half-naked boys, or tethered in pasture-grounds ...

Leaving Bileling, a pleasant sail of two days brought us to Ampanam in the island of Lombock ... We enjoyed superb views of the twin volcanoes of Bali and Lombock, each about eight thousand feet high, which form magnificent objects at sunrise and sunset, when they rise out of the mists and clouds that surround their bases ...

"The Malay Archipelago" (1869)

The dress of the women consists of a sarong, a wrap (badyu), a corset-like jacket (kutang) and a kind of shawl (slendang). Subdued colours, particularly shades of brown, are preferred. True sarongs, whose characteristic patterns are produced during dyeing by covering the parts not to be dyed with wax (the batik process), are often very valuable, costing 59 florins (guilders) or more.

Baedeker's "India" (1914)

Popular entertainments are the *wayang*, shadow plays performed by leather puppets behind a translucent screen, and the *wayang-orang*, mime plays with human actors wearing similar garb (gods and good spirits in gilded masks, princes and nobles in white ones, demons and devils in black ones). The plot is usually taken from the old Indian heroic legends and is explained by invisible narrators. Also popular are dances (*tandak*), which consist of artistic movements particularly of the hands and fingers. Strange and characteristic is the music of the *gamelangs* – orchestras of percussion instruments, gongs, cymbals and copper plates hanging from low frames, drums and a stringed instrument with two strings.

(Although this passage from Baedeker's 1914 guide refers to Java it can equally apply to Bali).

Hickman Powell

We were rolling down through the terraces, into the teeming, pregnant South. Everywhere were hills of coffee, coco groves, vast terraced vistas of rice. Dutch telephone wires straggled from planted poles that had sprouted, spread into flourishing trees. Everywhere was life. Ducks were swimming among the rice. About the villages were many swine, strange creatures weighted to collapse with their great loads of pork; their backbones sagged as if broken. Everywhere were cattle, with sweet-toned wooden bells – lithe agile animals that leaped upon the banks with all the grace of antelopes.

Everywhere was humanity. Roads streaming with girls. Heads proudly bearing burdens. Ankles, elbows, balanced curve of breast and armpit. Soft eyes, hair negligently hanging. Deep-shadowed backs of laden coolies. Breasts of aged, brittle women, and of fragile, unsexed children. Everywhere were swarming, seething. Life, surging in the market place beneath a massive banyan. Youths lolling by the roadside, fighting cocks brilliantly preening. High-held heads with baskets on them, chins curving into necks, and the tapering curve of fingers. Everywhere motion ...

"The Last Paradise" (1930)

Vicki Baum
Austrian writer
(1888–1960)

"Yes, there was pilfering and plundering. No doubt about that," the Resident said. "Cleaned out, in fact. It seems to me that the people of the coast went out with a real good will and reduced the ship to matchwood. The copper plates alone were worth five hundred guilders. It's true I can't get to the bottom of how much was carried off and how much simply went overboard when the ship struck, but it seems clear that at least one thousand one hundred and twenty-six guilders in money and goods have been stolen."

"In Badoeng," Boomsmer said. It sounded like the banging of a door. The Resident looked at him for a moment in silence and thought of something else.

"In Badoeng and Gianjar. To be accurate, more of the plunder was found on Gianjar territory than in Badoeng."

"The Government will not take much account of that," Boomsmer said with a smile.

"You may be sure of that. There would be no object in picking a quarrel with a province which is Dutch in any case. The Government will only want to establish one fact, and that is established already – that Bandoeng has violated Clause 11 of the Treaty of the 11th of July, 1849." ...

"These people could be brought to heel for good with two companies of soldiers," Boomsmer snapped ...

"I wish we could have settled the matter in a friendly way. I wish the lords of Bandoeng and Tabanan showed as much sense as our Gusti Njoman here. They can only be beaten and they know it. Why in the devil's name are they as obstinate as buffaloes?" [the Resident] said to himself ...

The misfortune that came to Pak's house began almost unnoticeably with sickness among his fowls. At first it was only two or three of the young black ones and then it spread to his whole flock. They sat with open beaks and would neither eat nor drink. His old father blew down their throats and pulled at their tongues, and his aunt compounded a medicine of poultry droppings and powdered chalk. But the fowls refused to swallow it, and after a few days their limp, dead bodies were found here and there in the corners of the yard.

Pak skinned one of the dead fowls and nailed it up with outstretched wings on the outside of the wall in order to keep the spirits from further mischief. But the sickness spread, and at last attacked even his lusty fighting-cocks in their bamboo basketwork cages, and this was indeed a cause for sorrow and alarm.

"A Tale from Bali" (1937)

Bali is a small and mountainous island lying to the west (*sic*) of Java. It has an area of about two thousand square miles, and about a million inhabitants. It can almost be described as the end of the Western world, for there is as much difference between the birds and quadrupeds on it and its neighbour Lombok (though they are separated only by a strait of fifteen miles) as there is between the fauna of England and Japan. In the last ten years this island has been written about, filmed, photographed, and gushed over to an extent which would justify nausea. I went there half-unwillingly, for I expected an uninteresting piece of bali-hoo, picturesque and faked to a Hollywood standard; I left wholly unwillingly, convinced that I had seen the nearest approach to Utopia that I am ever likely to see.

Geoffrey Gorer
English writer

"Bali and Angkor" (1936)

Even before we have driven across the island from north to south – between rice-fields in which people are ploughing and planting, past colourful little markets in which crowds of buyers are strolling round and the sellers are squatting by their wares, past innumerable villages, which here, very differently from Java, are separated from the road by high walls – even before we have reached our resting-place for the night, Den Pasar, I am completely under the spell of this country, under the spell of Bali and its own extraordinary beauty, still untouched, or almost untouched, by western influences. The "last paradise on earth" the Americans called it when they discovered the island a few years ago; and they were quite right! Thanks to the nearness of the sea it is hardly ever unbearably hot here. The colours are milder, the landscape lovelier than the grand scenery of Java. Everywhere on the mountain roads and in the valleys walk handsome, proud men and women with their animals – those patient grey buffaloes, white cows with deer-like heads, long files of ducks marching behind a small white flag as obediently as recruits ... And everywhere you observe what is lacking on Java: expressions of the people's deep commitment to their religion. The original animist faith of the Balinese has taken on a very distinctive character through the influence of Hinduism. For the ordinary Balinese – but not for the priestly caste – the world is peopled by gods, spirits and demons. The gods control birth and death, love and hate, good fortune and hardship; before any action or any enterprise the favour of the gods must be sought and the evil spirits warded off. In countless temples and in the little offering houses in the villages offerings of flowers and fruit are constantly being deposited ... Everywhere you meet women with quiet, serious faces carrying dishes containing offerings to a temple. Sometimes it will be an elaborately built-up pile of fruit, sometimes only a brown earthenware dish containing a few flowers or green sprigs ... For centuries it was the custom for girls and women to go about with bare bosoms: only immoral women were compelled to cover their breasts. In recent years, however, it has become increasingly the practice for women and girls to wear jackets – poor-quality cotton garments.

Jo(hanna) van
Ammers-Küller
Dutch writer
(1884–1966)

In the village schools children are required to wear trousers and skirts, though in the warm climate these are not at all necessary. If these influences continue to become more powerful on Bali, then in a few years the magnificent temples will stand empty and fall into decay, the Balinese will learn to regard their offerings as superstition, their dances as blasphemy and their cremations as barbarism, and of their fine culture there will remain only a few broken fragments and a memory ... On the Dutch people and their government there rests a heavy responsibility: to preserve the wondrous beauty of Bali unspoiled for posterity.

"The Indies: Experiences in the Dutch East Indies" (1940)

Suggested Routes

The routes suggested in this section are designed to help visitors exploring Bali in a hired car to plan their excursions, while leaving them free to vary the routes according to their particular interests and the time available.

If you are using public transport (buses, minibuses) you should allow plenty of time, since services and connections are very variable.

In view of Bali's small size any place on the island can be reached in a day trip, provided you start early in the morning and are prepared for a return in the late evening. For the circuit of the island two days are required.

One problem about driving on Bali is that the roads are not systematically numbered. In describing the following routes, therefore, reference is made wherever appropriate to compass directions or to the next town or village on the route. The kilometre stones along the roads show, in the one direction, the distance to Denpasar and in the other the distance to the next town or village.

The distances (in kilometres and miles) at the head of each route give the approximate total distance by the direct road. Where detours are suggested the distance (one way) is indicated.

You should bear in mind that the short distances indicated may be deceptive. On the one hand it is essential on the roads of Bali to drive slowly and with great care; and on the other you should allow plenty of time to enjoy the beauty of the scenery.

The routes suggested can be followed on the large map of Bali at the end of this guide.

In the description of the routes, places for which there is a separate entry in the A to Z section of the guide are shown in *bold* type. All the towns, villages, islands, regions and individual features of interest mentioned in the guide, whether the subject of a separate entry or not, are included in the Index at the end of the book.

1. Denpasar to Singaraja (1 day; round trip 220 km (135 mi.))

This is the most beautiful road on Bali, running through fascinating scenery with lively villages and friendly inhabitants. It also takes in some of the island's principal sights. An early start is essential.

From *Denpasar* take the road to Gilimanuk and in 40 km (25 mi.), at the village of Antosari, turn right into the road to Seririt.

Denpasar–Antosari (40 km (25 mi.))

From Antosari the road passes through a landscape of particular charm. At many points on this winding hill road there are astonishing views of the intricately patterned rice terraces. There are villages at frequent intervals, with schoolchildren and market women waving to the strangers and inns offering rest and refreshment.

Antosari–Pupuan (40 km (25 mi.))

Pupuan, the next place of any size, has no features of particular interest. The road continues to Seririt, on the north coast.
At Bubunan, shortly before Seririt, turn right into the road which runs east to *Singaraja*, Bali's second largest town. By now it will be about lunch-time, and there are a number of good restaurants in the town centre.

Pupuan–Singaraja (65 km (40 mi.))

The next sight to aim for is the lake temple of Pura Ulu Danu at *Bedugul*, on the road which goes south from Singaraja. On the way there a detour can be made to the Gitgit waterfall (see Singaraja, Surroundings). The

Singaraja–Bedugul (30 km (19 mi.))

71

temple is on the west side of Lake Bratan, just north of the village. If time permits it is worth visiting the beautiful Botanic Gardens at Bedugul before continuing south.

**Bedugul–
Denpasar
(25 km (15 mi.))**

Which route you choose for the return to Denpasar depends on the time available. If you leave Bedugul by about 3pm there is time to take the alternative route via Tabanan which is described below.
In the course of this day trip time is unlikely to permit a detour to the temple of Pura Luhur Batukau (see *Tabanan*). Instead it is recommended to end the day with a visit to the monkey forest of Sangeh (see *Mengwi*), taking the road from Pacung to Mengwi.

**Alternative
(44 km (27 mi.))**

Tabanan, once the capital of a powerful kingdom, is reached on a road which branches off the main road at Pacung and continues roughly parallel to it. The stretch of road between Badjera and Tabanan in particular runs through scenery of breathtaking beauty. Tabanan is famed for having one of the best gamelan orchestras on Bali. It also has a small museum (open only until 2pm) which gives an excellent survey of the history of rice-growing. From Tabanan it is only 21 km (13 mi.) on a good road to Denpasar.

2. Denpasar to Amlapura (1 day; round trip 180 km (112 mi.))

This day trip goes through eastern Bali, taking in a number of major sights. An early start is again advisable to leave time for seeing as much as possible.

**Denpasar–
Klungkung
(40 km (25 mi.))**

Leave *Denpasar* on the road which runs east to Celuk and Sukawati. The main road through *Celuk* is lined with silversmiths' and goldsmiths' shops. 17 km (11 mi.) from Denpasar is *Sukawati*, which has numerous

Rice terraces, Tabanan

Kerta Gosa (Court Hall), Klungkung

shops selling craft products. The town itself is of no particular interest, but there is an "art market" in the town centre in which prices are mostly lower than in the tourist centres around Denpasar.

The route continues through varied scenery to *Gianyar* and, 13 km (8 mi.) beyond this, *Klungkung*, with the magnificent Kerta Gosa (Court Hall).

From Klungkung the road leads south-east towards the sea and from Kusamba follows the coast. Directly on the road is the cave sanctuary of Goa Lawah (see Candi Dasa), with thousands of tiny bats at the entrance to the cave. From here it is only a few kilometres to *Candi Dasa*, the developing tourist centre in eastern Bali, which should be reached about lunch-time.

Klungkung–
Candi Dasa
(20 km (13 mi.))

Between Candi Dasa and Amlapura the road passes through many small villages. After briefly following the coast it turns inland and pursues a winding course through hills, with fine views at various points.

Candi Dasa–
Amlapura
(20 km (13 mi.))

One sight not to be missed in *Amlapura* (formerly Karangasem) is the princely palace of Puri Agung Kanginan with its beautiful pavilions, set in delightful gardens.

5 km (3 mi.) west of Amlapura are the Princely Baths of Tirthagangga (bathing). In clear weather Bali's highest mountain, Gunung Agung (3142 m (10,309 ft)), can be seen.

3. Round the Island (2 days; 450 km (280 mi.))

A complete circuit of Bali is to be recommended only for visitors interested in the less dramatically beautiful western part of the island. The main sight is the Bali Barat National Park; but the difficulty

Suggested Routes

here is that there are no roads negotiable by cars within the National Park.

Denpasar–
Tabanan
(22 km (14 mi.))

Leave Denpasar on the road which goes north-west to Gilimanuk. After passing through the attractive villages of Sempidi and Lukluk (with a number of interesting temples, brightly painted and richly decorated) it comes in 15 km (9 mi.) to *Kapal*, with the temples of Pura Desa and Pura Puseh. In the main street are a number of shops selling sacred figures cast in cement.

From Kapal it is only 7 km (4½ mi.) to *Tabanan*, chief town of Tabanan district, on a road running through varied scenery, which rises gradually towards the north of the island.

Tabanan itself has no features of particular interest, but there are a number of sights in the surrounding area.

Detour
(5 km (3 mi.))

A rewarding detour from Tabanan is to the little village of Krambitan, to the south-west, with two former princely palaces, Puri Gede and Puri Anyur. Puri Gede is now a very beautiful hotel which, with only a small number of rooms, is almost always fully booked.

Tabanan–
Negara
(75 km (47 mi.))

The road now continues west along the coast to *Negara*, passing on the way the little town of Pulukan, with beautiful sandy beaches which are inviting for bathers. Negara itself is noted mainly for the water-buffalo races held annually in November. If you arrive in Negara at the right time of year it is well worth while staying to see the races.

Negara–
Gilimanuk
(33 km (21 mi.))

Beyond Negara the road continues close to the coast, with the Bali Barat National Park to the right. The headquarters of the National Park administration, where tickets are sold for admission to the park, are at Cecik, shortly before Gilimanuk.

Gilimanuk has no features of interest worth mentioning. It is worth while pausing briefly – but, with some distance still to travel, not too long – to watch the busy activity in the harbour, from which there is a ferry to Java.

Gilimanuk–
Terima
(10 km (6 mi.)

The road between Gilimanuk and Terima is the only road in the Bali Barat National Park (see *Terima*) suitable for vehicles. It is worth while driving slowly along this short stretch to enjoy the extraordinary beauty of the scenery. Terima itself has little of interest to offer, but if time permits it is worth taking the half-hour boat trip to the island of Manjangan (good bathing, snorkelling and scuba diving).

Terima–
Singaraja
(85 km (53 mi.))

The road which runs east along the coast via Seririt to Singaraja is relatively featureless and of little interest. Shortly before reaching Singaraja it passes through the well equipped tourist resort of Lovina Beach. Here the road is lined with hotels, restaurants and shops.

During the period of Dutch rule *Singaraja* was the seat of the colonial government and thus in effect the capital of Bali. It is now the island's second largest town. In order to allow sufficient time for seeing the town and its principal sights (Pura Dalem, Gedong Kirtya Library) it is advisable to spend the night either in Singaraja itself or in Lovina Beach.

Singaraja–
Amlapura
(140 km (87 mi.))

An early start is recommended the next morning, both to observe the people of Singaraja starting the day and to allow plenty of time for seeing the sights in and around Amlapura.

Detour
(10 km (6 mi.))

A very beautiful road (signposted to Bedugul) runs south from Singaraja to the Gitgit waterfall.

The road to Amlapura continues east along the coast and then turns inland, passing through an intensively cultivated region, with the largest coffee plantations on Bali. From Singaraja it is a four hours' drive to *Amlapura*.

Amlapura (formerly called Karangasem) suffered heavy destruction in the last eruption of Gunung Agung on March 17th 1963, and new modern functional buildings were erected on the ruins of the old town. Here and there, however, there are still blackened walls and ruined houses – mute testimony to a devastating natural catastrophe. Two sights not to be missed are the princely palace of Puri Agung Kanginan, which survived the disaster, and the princely baths of Tirthagangga.

The distance between Amlapura and Klungkung is only 40 km (25 mi.), but time should be allowed for enjoying the scenery of this particularly beautiful part of Bali. For part of the way the road runs through hilly country, with fine views of the sea at some points.

Amlapura–
Klungkung
(40 km (25 mi.))

A short distance beyond the well equipped tourist centre of *Candi Dasa*, directly on the road, is the cave temple of Goa Lawah, one of the most important sanctuaries on Bali. The site can be identified from some distance away by the tourist coaches parked outside. Perhaps the most striking feature is the sight of thousands of tiny bats clinging to the bare rock at the entrance to the cave.

From Goa Lawah it is only 12 km (7½ mi.) to *Klungkung*, famed particularly for the Kerta Gosa (Court Hall) with its paintings in Wayang style.

On the last stage of the route the road passes through a number of villages and small towns. If you want to reach *Denpasar* by the evening of the second day there is little time for further sightseeing. Within easy reach of Denpasar, however, are *Gianyar*, *Sukawati* and *Celuk*, with interesting temples and other sights, which can be seen in half-day trips.

Klungkung–
Denpasar
(40 km (25 mi.))

**Reiseziele
von A bis Z**

Region: East Bali
District: Karangasem
Altitude: 2–90 m (6–295 ft)

Access

By road: Denpasar to Sakah; then bear right for Blahbatuh and
Klungkung; from there along the coast, via Candi Dasa.
Bus: several times daily from Denpasar-Kereneng.
Bemo (see Practical Information, Public Transport): good services along
the road.

Amlapura (formerly called Karangasem), the administrative centre of
Karangasem district, is the most easterly town on Bali, situated at the
foot of the Gunung Agung volcano. It is some 80 km (50 mi.) from
Denpasar.

History Amlapura, known as Karangasem until 1964, played an important part during the years when the Dutch were attempting to gain a
foothold on Bali. While the rulers of the princedoms of central Bali were
for the most part preparing to resist the threatened occupation, the Rajas
of Karangasem reached an accommodation with the occupying forces
and thus left the eastern part of the island exposed. The Dutch were then
able to sail round the south coast to Sanur and attack the princes of
Gianyar and Badung, who were still holding out against them, near their
capitals. The Dutch were duly grateful: Karangasem became one of the
wealthiest towns on Bali and the Raja retained his power.
Amlapura was devastated by the eruption of Gunung Agung on March
17th 1963 – not so much by the flows of lava, which did not reach the
town, as by the earthquakes accompanying the eruption, which
destroyed almost every building in the town. For some years Amlapura
also suffered from the destruction of almost all the main roads linking it
with the rest of the island, and it is only since the late seventies that it
has again been served by good roads. Since then the town has taken on
a fresh lease of life and developed into a modest district centre.

The scars left by the 1963 eruption can still be seen. A walk about the
town will reveal the ruins of houses which have been wholly or partly
destroyed and are only gradually being replaced by new building.

Sights

★Puri Agung
Kanginan

Open during
daylight

Admission charge

On the road to Ujung is the late 19th century princely palace of Puri
Agung Kanginan. Although part of it was destroyed in the 1963 earthquakes it is still well worth a visit.
The palace consists of three parts. In the first part, called Bengingah, the
traditional festivals were held; in the second are the gardens; and in the
third and innermost part are the residential apartments of the princely
family.
 The palace complex, which is rather crowded with buildings, is
entered through a gate on a square base, guarded by lions. Beyond the
ticket office, to the right, is another gate leading into the gardens and
then into the main palace precinct. On the right is an artificial pond with
a pavilion, the Bale Kambang, and to the left of this another *bale* decorated with numerous scenes from the "Ramayana".
 Within the main palace precinct are a number of notable buildings.
The Bale London (so called because of the British royal crest on the furniture) has richly carved doors and well preserved (or restored) paint-

◀ *The landscape of Bali is marked by innumerable elaborately laid out rice terraces.*

In the Puri Agung Kanginan

Bale Kambang in the Puri Agung Kanginan

ings on the outer walls and in the interior (explanatory leaflet obtainable at ticket office) and contains the instruments of a gamelan orchestra, which could be played only in presence of the Raja. Beside the Bale London is the Bale Pemandesan, in which the ritual tooth-filing was performed on the Raja's children. The Puri Madura (Audience Hall), also known as the Maskerdam, can accommodate 150 people. It has been closed since the death of the last occupant, Prince A. A. Angurah Ketut Karangasem, in 1966, but it is possible to look in through the windows. Outside the palace complex, across the main road, are a number of other buildings, some of which belong to the Puri Agung, others to two old palaces, the Puri Gede and Puri Kertasura. Some of the buildings were destroyed by earthquakes.

Surroundings

★**Tirthagangga**

Open daily
9am–6pm

Admission charge

5 km (3 mi.) west of Amlapura are the former princely baths of Tirthagangga ("Water of the Ganges"), which are now an open-air swimming pool open to the public. The baths, constructed by the last Raja of Amlapura about 1947, are beautifully laid out, with fountains, statues and figures of fabulous beasts. They were damaged during the 1963 eruption but have been restored as far as possible to their original form.

Ujung

There is another "water palace" at Ujung, also built by the last Raja of Amlapura, on the coast 5 km (3 mi.) south of Amlapura. It suffered extensive destruction in the 1963 earthquakes and little is left of the original buildings.

★**Scenery** Between Candi Dasa and Amlapura the road runs through a hilly tropical landscape of extraordinary charm. The area round Amlapura is intensively cultivated, with great expanses of terraced rice-fields.

Princely Baths, Tirthagangga

Bali Barat National Park

See Terima

Bangli   N 6

Region: Central Bali
District: Bangli
Altitude: 392 m (1286 ft)

By road: from Denpasar north-east via Sukawati to Sakah, then turn right   Access
into the road to Blahbatuh and continue via Gianyar to Bangli (watch out
for signposts).
Bus: excellent regular services from Denpasar-Kereneng.
Bemo: Denpasar to Gianyar, then change for Bangli.

Bangli, chief town of one of the nine administrative districts (kabupaten)
of Bali, was once an independent princedom. A little to the north of the
town are the foothills of the Gunung Agung volcano.
The town itself lies 39 km (25 mi.) north-east of Denpasar at the upper
end of the well watered central uplands, in good and productive agricultural country. The crater lake of Batur, Bali's largest lake, lies within
the area of the town.

History The town of Bangli, now one of the cultural centres of Bali, first
appears in the records in 1204, when a great religious festival was celebrated here. Later Bangli became capital of an independent princedom,
though its rulers never enjoyed great influence, looking to the powerful
Rajas of Klungkung for help or protection when required.

Sights

The **town** of Bangli is dominated by the magnificent backdrop of Mt
Batur, which is particularly impressive in the morning; later in the day it
is almost always capped with clouds.
In the town itself there are a series of interesting temples, five of them
dedicated to the powers of the underworld.

Every three days a large **market** is held in front of the Raja's palace, Puri
Artha Sastra, in the centre of the town, at which peasants from the surrounding area sell their produce.

The former palace of the Raja of Bangli, the Puri Artha Sastra, was con-   ★ Puri Artha
verted some years ago into a small hotel, the owner of which is the   Sastra
young Raja himself.
    The *bales* are decorated with traditional Balinese and with Chinese
paintings. In the attractive grounds are a number of statues and figures
from Hindu mythology. A large and imposing gate leads into the interior
of the palace; on either side of the gate are fine reliefs.

The Pura Kehen (Temple of the Treasury), some 2.5 km (1½ mi.) north of   ★ Pura Kehen
the town centre, is one of the largest and finest temples on Bali. Built on
seven terraces below the hill of Bukit Bangli, it was founded in the 11th
century by the princely priest Sri Brahma Kemute Ketu. It contains valuable bronze tablets believed to date from 1204, the year in which Bangli
was founded.
    The first four terraces lead up to a covered gate (*candi korung*) at the
entrance to the main temple precinct. To the right of this, in the outer

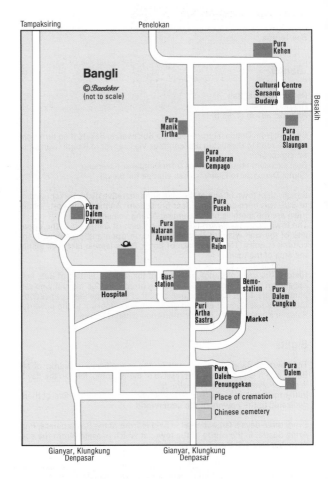

Tampaksiring   Penelokan

Bangli

© *Baedeker*
(not to scale)

Besakih

Pura Kehen

Cultural Centre
Sarsana
Budaya

Pura Manik Tirtha

Pura Dalem Slaungan

Pura Panataran Cempago

Pura Dalem Purwa

Pura Puseh

Pura Nataran Agung

Pura Rajan

Hospital

Bus-station

Bemo-station

Pura Dalem Cungkub

Puri Artha Sastra

Market

Pura Dalem Penunggekan

Pura Dalem

Place of cremation

Chinese cemetery

Gianyar, Klungkung
Denpasar

Gianyar, Klungkung
Denpasar

forecourt, is a *bale* for the gamelan orchestra; to the right another *bale* is now an assembly point for visitors to the temple.

In the centre of the outer forecourt stands the Batu Keramat, a stone which is venerated as sacred. On the far side of the forecourt steps lead up to the split gate (*candi bentar*) at the entrance to the inner forecourt, on the next terrace. Beyond the gate, to right and left, are two buildings in which shadow plays are performed during temple festivals. Set into the wall on the far side of the forecourt are pieces of faience of Chinese origin.

Another split gate leads into the innermost and most sacred part of the temple, on the far side of which (the side nearest the hill) are a number of *merus* with varying numbers of tiers (the tallest, with eleven tiers, being dedicated to Shiva), shrines for various divinities and *tugus* (stone lanterns which are the abode of divinities of lower rank).

By road: from Denpasar via Sukawati and Sakah; then shortly before Ubud, at Teges, take a road on the right.
Bus and bemo: good regular services from Denpasar-Kereneng.

Bedulu, once capital of the oldest princedom on Bali, lies in an intensively cultivated region which rises gradually from here to the central uplands. Over the years Bedulu has gradually joined up with the neighbouring town of Pejeng.

In Bedulu itself there are no sights of particular interest: these are to be found in the neighbouring town of Pejeng (see below) and in the surrounding area. One feature that may catch the eye in passing through the town is the four-headed divine figure at the street intersection in the centre of the town.

Surroundings

1 km (¾ mi.) south of Bedulu is the source sanctuary of Yeh Pulu, with a relief 27 m (89 ft) long and up to 2 m (6½ ft) high, believed to be one of the oldest on Bali, depicting scenes from everyday life on the island. Archaeologists are divided about the meaning and purpose of this relief: some of the scenes may depict Krishna or refer to legends about one of his numerous manifestations. The figures, which are life-size and fully rounded, probably date from the 14th or 15th century.

★★**Yeh Pulu**

Goa Gajah

Ubud

Bedulu, Gianyar

Car park

Elephant Cave
a Elephant god Ganesha
b Three lingams

Hariti pavilion

Large pavilion

Bathing place

Pura Taman

Meditation niche

Fragments of candi

Buddha statues

© Baedeker
(not to scale)

Petanu

★★**Goa Gajah**

2 km (1¼ mi.) from Bedulu the famous Elephant Cave of Goa Gajah was revered by Hindus from the end of the first millennium and possibly by Buddhists before then. The cave was rediscovered in 1923, and the bathing-place in front of it was excavated in 1954. This source sanctuary owes its name – unexpected on Bali, where according to tradition there were never any elephants – to the form of the cave mouth, which looks something like an elephant's head. In the cave is revered a 1 m (3 ft) high figure with four arms representing the elephant god Ganesha, one of the sons of Shiva. To the right of this, on a stone base, are three lingams, symbolising Shiva in his three manifestations as Brahma, Vishnu and Shiva himself. Round each lingam are eight

Ritual bathing-places at the Goa Gajah

Entrance to the Elephant Cave

small phallic symbols, representing the eight guardians of the worlds. Outside the cave were separate bathing pools for men and for women, with a small one in between whose function is not known (possibly for the ritual purification of members of the priestly caste). The pipes from which the water emerged are elaborately carved.

To see the Elephant Cave properly you should have a pocket torch (not available locally).

Near the Elephant Cave is the temple of Pura Samuan Tiga, which is dedicated to the Hindu trinity of Brahma, Vishnu and Shiva. It contains a number of shrines housing particularly venerated figures.

**Pura
Samuan Tiga**

At the east end of Bedulu, on the road to Pejeng, stands the very interesting Archaeological Museum (Gedong Arca Purbakala).

★★**Gedong Arca
Purbakala**

In the inner courtyard are 53 tufa sarcophagi of varying size which are believed to date from about 300 BC. They were found in the early seventies on 37 different sites on Bali and brought together here. Some of them show signs of damage – probably the work of tomb-robbers or careless excavators.

Open mornings

Admission charge

The dead were laid in the sarcophagi not in the traditional western fashion but in a crouching posture. This is thought to be a symbolic representation of the eternal cycle of birth, death and rebirth, in which the dead person was reborn from a foetal position. Particularly striking is a sarcophagus found at Taman Bali (near Bangli) in the form of two turtles (symbols of the underworld), one on top of the other. Interestingly, the head of the lower turtle has human features.

The museum displays a variety of jewellery and ornaments, utensils and implements dating from the Stone and Bronze Ages – mostly chance finds rather than the result of planned excavation. Of particular interest are the miniature stupas from the Bedulu/Pejeng area, no doubt dating from Bali's Buddhist period (8th–10th c. AD).

200 m (220 yds) farther along the road, on the left, is the Pura Kebo Edan, the Temple of the Crazy Water-Buffalo. In the centre of the temple can be seen a colossal figure 3.60 m (12 ft) high, thought to represent the giant Bhairava, standing on a figure who is probably Yama, god of the dead. To left and right are a bull and a giant demon.

★**Pura Kebo Edan**

On the *bales* are numerous figures and fragments, many of them with terrifyingly grimacing faces. It is believed that orgiastic Tantric ceremonies were celebrated in this temple, in the course of which the participants are said to have drunk human blood.

★★Pura Panataran Sasih

The principal sight in the temple of Pura Panataran Sasih, which stands on the road from Bedulu to Pejeng, is what is claimed to be the largest kettledrum in the world, the famous "**Moon of Pejeng**". In fact it is not so much a drum as a gong, 1.25 m (4 ft) in diameter and richly decorated with spiral bands of ornament, stylised faces and Hindu symbols. Little can be seen of this, however, since the gong is hung high up in a bale and partly concealed.

While the date of the gong is well established (Dongsong culture, c. 300 BC), it has not been possible, in spite of intensive research, to determine its place of origin or the meaning of the decoration. The local people are firmly of the opinion that the Moon of Pejeng was one of the originally thirteen moons in the sky and that it fell to earth on the precise spot where the temple now stands. It is said that on the night on which it fell it landed in the branches of a tree, where it shone so brightly that it upset the plans of a gang of thieves. One of the thieves tried to put the light out by urinating on it: whereupon the moon exploded, killing the thief, and fell to the ground.

Benoa

See Bukit Badung Peninsula

Besakih   O 5

Region: Central Bali
District: Karangasem
Altitude: 980–1011 m (3215–3317 ft)

Access

By road: from Denpasar north-east to Klungkung, then north to Rendang
and Besakih (approx. 63 km (39 mi.)).
Bus: regular bus service only to Klungkung; from there bemos.
Bemo: not recommended from Denpasar; from Klungkung and Rendang
good services (sometimes necessary to charter the whole bemo).

Although the village of Besakih is of no interest in itself, it lies near the
Pura Besakih (royal temple), the "first and holiest" temple on Bali.

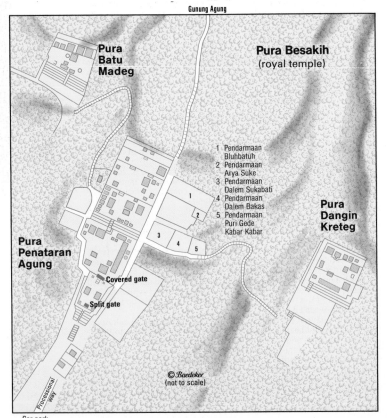

Gunung Agung

Pura
Batu
Madeg

Pura Besakih
(royal temple)

1 Pendarmaan
  Bluhbatuh
2 Pendarmaan
  Arya Suke
3 Pendarmaan
  Dalem Sukabati
4 Pendarmaan
  Dalem Bakas
5 Pendarmaan
  Puri Gede
  Kabar Kabar

Pura
Dangin
Kreteg

Pura
Penataran
Agung

Covered gate

Split gate

© Baedeker
(not to scale)

Processional Way

Car park

★★Pura Besakih

In the car park at the entrance to the temple Balinese of all ages offer their services as **guides**. Usually they speak very little English and know only the main facts about the temple. If you do hire a guide the price should be agreed in advance (about 10,000 rupiahs).

The temple, laid out on terraces and built mainly of dark-coloured lava stone, may strike visitors as unimpressive – unless they come at the time of the annual temple festival, in which tens of thousands of Hindus from all over the island and from farther afield take part. There are more colourful and more elaborately decorated temples on Bali, but to the Hindus none is so important as the Pura Besakih, the "Mother of All Temples".

In addition to its annual "birthday" festival (the *odalan* festival) the Pura Besakih is the scene of Bali's most important temple festival, the **Eka Dasa Rudra**, which is celebrated every hundred years.
  The festival last took place in 1979. This was a departure from the usual timing, and for good reason. The festival was due to be celebrated in 1963, but the preparations were interrupted by the eruption in that year of Gunung Agung, previously thought to be extinct. Over 2500 people were killed and many villages in the surrounding area were destroyed. The Eka Dasa Rudra festival, therefore, was put off until 1979.

Location The Pura Besakih (whose name is probably derived from the snake Basuki which features in Hindu mythology) lies in a luxuriant tropical landscape at the foot of Gunung Agung, which forms a magnificent backdrop, particularly in the clear morning light.

The temple complex of Pura Besakih

Merus in the Pura Besakih

History The Pura Besakih is thought to have been originally founded in the 8th century AD, possibly as a Buddhist shrine, since at that time Bali had not yet been converted to Hinduism. Tradition tells of a priest of Shiva named Sri Markhadeya who founded a temple on this spot. The main parts of the present temple were probably built in the 10th century by the local ruler Kesari Warmadewa.

Some parts of the temple are usually (particularly during preparations for the temple festival) closed to non-Hindus. A well signposted path, which visitors may not leave, runs through the temple precinct.

Temple precinct Below the temple is a large car park, beyond which all motor traffic is prohibited. From here a wide avenue leads up to the temple, lined with shops selling religious articles and souvenirs. Then on the left is seen the first of a total of 15 family temples – a number which is likely to increase, for when a Balinese family rise to some consequence they like to have their own family or ancestral temple within the precincts of the Pura Besakih.

A broad flight of steps and a split gate (*candi bentar*) lead into the first of five temple precincts, separated from one another by lava walls of varying height. In the corners to left and right of the gate are bell-towers (*kulkul*). In the first precinct, in adjoining walled courtyards, are a number of secular buildings in which offerings are prepared before the great temple festival. Visitors who are fortunate enough to arrive a few days before a festival will be able to watch these preparations.

Standing at an angle to the wall is a building in which the priests prepare holy water and distribute it to worshippers. Then a further flight of steps and a covered gate (*padur raksa*) lead into the second temple precinct.

A small donation is expected from visitors

In the third precinct, to the left, are four *merus* with varying numbers of tiers (*tumpangs*); the tallest has seven.

Beyond this, outside the actual precinct, is a small temple dedicated to the smiths' guild. The fact that the smiths had their own temple in the Pura Besakih indicates the predominant importance of this trade on Bali. The most important and holiest precinct of the Pura Besakih contains relatively few buildings. At the near end are two *merus*, an eleven-tiered one on the right and a three-tiered one on the left, and beyond these are other sacred buildings. From the terrace there is a fine view of the whole temple area.

Various princely families or their descendants are responsible for the upkeep of the shrines in the main part of the complex, the Pura Panataran Agung: the Rajas of Bangli for the shrine of Vishnu, the Rajas of Karangasem (Amlapura) for that of Brahma, the Rajas of Klungkung for that of Shiva.

There are other shrines outside the temple precincts. The Pura Dangin Kreteg is reached on a path which goes off to the right of the Pura Penataran Agung, and above it, to the left, is the Pura Batu Madeg.

★★Gunung Agung

There are various routes to the summit of Gunung Agung, Bali's highest mountain and the abode of Shiva, not only from Besakih but also from Amlapura (about 6 hours) and Sebudi, near Selat (about 7 hours). In this section only the south-westerly route from Besakih is described. This is for fit climbers only, for since there are no mountain huts in which to spend the night it is necessary to do the ascent and descent in one day (at night and in the early morning it can be decidedly cold!).

Stout footwear, weatherproof clothing and sufficient supplies of food and water are essential.

On this volcanic terrain it is dangerous to leave the signposted route, and even experienced climbers should take a local guide.

A very early start is advisable, preferably about 2am. Good climbers will take between six and nine hours for the ascent; the descent takes at least five hours. The climb begins at the principal temple in the Pura Besakih. The first part, through dense forest, is relatively gentle, but later it becomes much steeper. After about five hours a rock wall known as the Kori Agung and regarded as the gateway to the summit region is reached. From here it is another two or three hours to the rim of the crater, the walls of which drop steeply down for up to 100 m (330 ft). This even more strenuous climb is rewarded by fascinating views over much of the island.

Bukit Badung Peninsula   K/L 10/11

Region: South Bali
District: Badung
Altitude: 0–200 m (660 ft)

Access

By road: 21 km (13 mi.) from Denpasar on the Jalan Bypass; 15 km (9 mi.) from Kuta and Legian, 23 km (14 mi.) from Sanur.
Bus: regular services from Denpasar-Tegal.
Bemo: on road between Denpasar and Nusa Dua.

Taxi: registered taxis between Denpasar, Kuta, Legian and Sanur. Drivers often suggest, particularly in the evening and at night, switching off the meter and then name a fixed price – on which haggling is perfectly in order.

Pagodas of the Pura Luhur Ulu Watu, high above the sea

Bukit Badung is the peninsula at the south end of Bali, linked with the rest of the island by an isthmus only 1.7 km (1 mi.) across at its widest point.

Originally the peninsula had little of interest to offer. The barren soil was unsuitable for farming, and fishing provided a living for only a few of the inhabitants. It is only since the mid seventies of this century that the development of the tourist centre at Nusa Dua has made Bukit Badung widely known.

Sights

High above an 80 m (260 ft) high cliff falling sheer down to the sea, near the village of Pecatu, is the temple of Pura Luhur Ulu Watu. It is reached on a road which branches off the Jalan Bypass (round Denpasar) and runs south-west. It is 4 km (2½ mi.) from Pecatu to the site.

★ ★ **Pura Luhur Ulu Watu** (usually closed)

The temple ranks as one of the most important on Bali and has the status of a royal temple (Sadkahyangan). Dedicated to the goddess Rudra (one of the manifestations of Shiva), it is oriented towards the sea. Its most notable features are the richly decorated gates, which, like the other structures of the temple, are built of coralline limestone.

From the entrance to the temple precincts there is a superb view of the sea and, at high tide, of the heavy surf lashing against the much eroded cliffs.

In the tourist centre of Nusa Dua on the east coast of the peninsula luxury hotels nestle in beautiful tropical gardens. After the construction of the Nusa Dua Beach Hotel it was decided that no new hotel should be higher than the tallest palms in the neighbourhood. Thanks to the strict observance of this rule and to the architects' concern to follow the traditional Balinese style of building this new tourist development with its extensive lawns and parks fits harmoniously and elegantly into the landscape.

Nusa Dua

On the road between Denpasar and the Bukit Badung peninsula, at the beginning of the tourist area, is a large split gate (*candi bentar*) – perhaps symbolically marking an invisible line of separation between Balinese and tourists, a passage from one world to another?

On the north-eastern edge of the peninsula extends the long, narrow

Benoa

Pura Luhur Ulu Watu
(royal temple)

Indian Ocean

Inner courtyard — Middle courtyard — Outer courtyard — Entrance

Vishnu
Dwijendra — Brahma

1 *Candi bentar* (split gate)
2 *Candi korung* (covered gate)
3 *Aling-aling* (protective wall against demons)
4 *Meru* (tiered pagoda)

© *Baedeker*
(not to scale)

Cliffs on the Bukit Badung peninsula

promontory of Benoa, opposite which is the little port of the same name (boats to the "Turtle Island" of Nusa Penida).

Buleleng

See Singaraja

Candi Dasa   P 7

Region: East Bali
District: Karangasem
Altitude: sea level

Access

By road: Denpasar to Sakah, turn right to Blahbatuh and Klungkung, then along the coast via Padang Bai.
Bus: several times daily from Denpasar-Kereneng.
Bemo: good services along road.

Candi Dasa, which during the last few years has been developed as a tourist centre, lies on the coast 20 km (13 mi.) south-west of Amlapura, on the busy road to eastern Bali.

The Resort

Until a few years ago Candi Dasa, at the east end of Labuhan Amuk Bay,

On the seafront, Candi Dasa

was a remote little fishing village known only to a few holidaymakers, mainly backpackers. Since then it has developed into a lively holiday centre which has nevertheless contrived to remain unspoiled. There are no top-category hotels as there are at Nusa Dua, but the facilities for visitors are more than adequate. Visitors who want a quiet holiday, away from the hectic activity of a city like Denpasar, are well catered for in Candi Dasa.

A handicap of this resort, which has grown at such an unnaturally rapid pace, is the state of its sandy beach. Since the coast is exposed with relatively little protection to the action of surf which at times can be extremely strong, the sand has simply been swept away. This was largely the result of the uncontrolled quarrying of the offshore banks of coral (used in the production of lime), and although the government prohibited this activity the ban came too late, so that Candi Dasa now has only a very narrow strip of beach. The hotel-owners have had to protect their beaches, at considerable expense, by building stone barrier walls.

Surroundings

Half way between Klungkung and Candi Dasa, near the village of Kusamba, is the cave sanctuary of Goa Lawah (Bat Cave), one of the six royal temples on Bali. It is highly revered by the Balinese, largely because of the belief that there is an underground passage linking the cave (which has not yet been explored to its farthest point) with the island's holiest temple, the Pura Besakih, and thus marking the point of junction between the upper world and the underworld; for Goa Lawah is believed to be the abode of Sangyang Basuki, one of the two snakes of the underworld. In the mouth of the cave is a lotus throne (*padmasana*) reserved for Basuki.

★★Goa Lawah

The cave is home to countless thousands of tiny bats, who cling in dense masses to the walls and the mouth of the cave.

To the right of the entrance to the cave is a small temple with several wooden *merus* to which the local people bring offerings every two weeks, receiving in return holy water which is used in various ceremonies, for example in the rice-fields in the surrounding area.

Balina Beach

4 km (2½ mi.) from Candi Dasa on the road to Klungkung lies Balina Beach, a new tourist resort which has been developed in the last few years. The sand here is lighter in colour than at Candi Dasa.

Padang Bai

At the west end of Labuhan Amuk Bay is the ferry port of Padang Bai, from which there are services to the offshore islands and to Lombok (see entry). Here too anchor the large cruising liners which include Bali in their programme.

Tenganan

See entry

Celuk   M 8

Region: Central Bali
District: Gianyar
Altitude: 100 m (330 ft)

Access

By road: 12 km (7½ mi.) from Denpasar on the Sukawati road.
Bus: regular services daily from Denpasar–Kereneng.
Bemo: from Denpasar, Ubud and Mas and on Sukawati road.

There are several places called Celuk on Bali. The one described here is the craftsmen's village of Celuk near Sukawati, 12 km (7½ mi.) from Denpasar.

Craftsmen's village

Along the main street of the long, straggling village of Celuk are numerous **goldsmiths'** and **silversmiths'** shops, some of them with workshops which can be visited. Prices are about the same as in the tourist centres, for Celuk is on the regular route of the organised coach tours.
Many of the shops offer to make items of jewellery "to measure", though they require up to a week for this. Before paying you should check the quality of the work.

Celuk is also famed for its **woodcarvers**, particularly those who make *wayang* figures and *topeng* masks. The work is usually based on traditional models, but some of the *wayang* figures are of the type produced on the neighbouring island of Java. It should be borne in mind that many of the masks are mass-produced for tourists.

There are other craftsmen's shops in the villages around Celuk, for example in Guang, Batuan and Sukawati. With luck you may still find craftsmen in these villages who take the trouble to produce careful and conscientious work.

Denpasar   M 8

Region: South Bali
District: Badung

Popular souvenirs: carved wooden masks

Altitude: 40 m (130 ft)
Population: about 300,000

Denpasar (Badung), or rather its airport at Ngurah Rai, is usually the point of arrival for visitors to Bali. Since the completion of the four-lane Jalan Bypass, however, they are likely to see little of the city itself as they head right away for one of the tourist resorts.

Denpasar has been the island's chief town and administrative centre, the seat of the governor of the province of Bali, since 1936, when it took over these functions from Singaraja (see entry) in the north of the island. In that year, too, it took the name of Denpasar ("New Market"): previously it had been called Badung, like the district in which it lies. The local people still refer to their town as Badung.

Development Since the 1960s Denpasar has enjoyed a massive boom, one of the consequences of which has been an alarmingly high concentration of population in and around the city. There are now over 930 people to the sq. km (2410 to the sq. mile) in this area, compared with 250 to the sq. km (650 to the sq. mile) in the western part of the island.
    The problems now facing Denpasar are enormous – bad air, environmental pollution, dense traffic and too many people hoping to earn their living in the tourist centres within easy reach of the capital. As a result Denpasar is expanding ever farther and at many points is joining up with independent townships in its immediate surroundings.

History The Raja of Badung was one of the first rulers to accept colonial rule, and signed a treaty to this effect in 1841. He hoped that this would lead the Dutch to leave the province of Badung undisturbed and allow him a degree of independence. And so it proved for a period of 63 years,

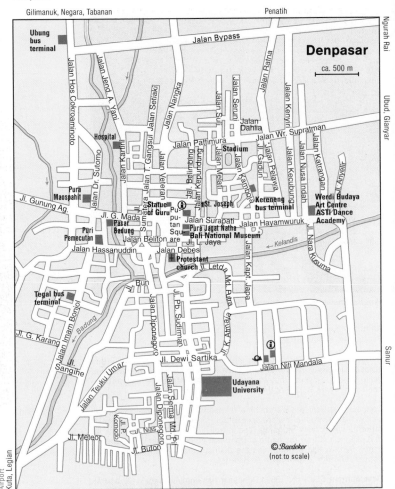

Gilimanuk, Negara, Tabanan   Penatih

Ngurah Rai

Denpasar

ca. 500 m

Ubud, Gianyar

Sanur

Airport
Kuta, Legian

Benoa Harbour

until an unfortunate incident in 1904. On the night of May 27th in that year the Chinese schooner "Sri Kumala" ran aground on the coast off Denpasar. The vessel was looted by the Balinese, whereupon the owner claimed compensation, at first from Raja Agung Made and later, when this produced no result, from the Dutch. After fruitless negotiations the Dutch presented an ultimatum to the Raja and proceeded to throw siege lines round Denpasar. When the Raja declared that he would not give in to the ultimatum they drew the ring more tightly round the town and prepared on September 14th 1906 to take it.

Subsequent events on that day have etched the period of Dutch colonial rule indelibly in the memory of the Balinese. When the Dutch forces marched on the Raja's palace the gates opened and a long train of people, headed by the Raja himself in a litter, advanced slowly to meet the invaders. The procession came to a halt only a few yards from the Dutch, and a Brahman priest took the Raja's jewel-encrusted kris and plunged it in his master's heart. This example was followed by all the others, and men, women and children all met their death in the same way. The Dutch forces were at first taken aback by this turn of events, but then took up their weapons and shot those Balinese who had not died in this ritual mass suicide (*puputan*). The palace was set on fire and almost completely destroyed.

The example set by the Raja of Badung and his people was followed on the same day by the Raja of Pemecutan and later by the Raja of Tabanan, whom the Dutch had thrown into prison in Badung. In 1908 there was a similar *puputan* in Klungkung in which 250 people died.

Thereafter the Dutch were exposed to increased international pressure, and in 1914 they replaced their military forces by a detachment of police.

Sights

Seeing the places of interest in Denpasar on foot is not to be recommended. For one thing the individual sights tend to be some distance apart and are most easily visited by taxi; and in any case a walk through the noisy and crowded streets of the city is a torment rather than a pleasure.

The palace of the Rajas of Badung (Puri Pemecutan), now a pleasant small hotel, lies in the angle between Jalan Thamrin and Jalan Hassannudin. Behind a red brick wall are a number of charming buildings set in a luxuriant tropical garden. The contrast could hardly be starker:

★★Rajas of Badung

Open daily 8am–5pm

Admission charge

Pavilion in the Puri Pemecutan

outside the palace are clamorous traffic and swarms of people, while inside it cocks in wicker baskets crow in peaceful rivalry with one another.

The palace was almost completely burned down after the *puputan* on September 14th 1906, but a year later was rebuilt by the Dutch, though not on its original scale. Notable features are the richly decorated entrance gate and – the only relics of the original palace – a number of fine reliefs towards the rear of the palace precinct. In one building is a collection of *lontar* (palm-leaf) books which survived the fire, in another some old gamelan instruments.

★★Bali National Museum

Open Tue.–Thu. 8am–2pm, Fri. 8–11am, Sat. 8am– 12.30pm, Sun. 8am–2pm

Admission charge

Although the Bali National Museum, measured by the standards of other national museums, may fall short in the matter of systematic arrangement, it is well worth a visit. Most of the exhibits now have labels in English explaining their history, origin and significance. A guide to the museum in English is advertised at the ticket-office but is usually out of print.

The Museum, in Jalan Wisnu, near Puputan Square (whose name recalls the events of September 14th 1906), is housed in three adjoining buildings in traditional Balinese style or rebuilt on the model of the original palace. They lie in a special precinct within the palace complex, entered through a split gate (*candi bentar*). Another split gate on the street which runs past the precinct is always closed. Beside it is a bell-tower (*kulkul*).

The best place to start a tour of the museum is the rear building, where the exhibits include a glass case containing tableaux of a wedding (front) and a tooth-filing ceremony (rear); various wooden models, including a royal throne; carved symbols of Hindu divinities; batik work and embroidery. Also of interest are the finely carved shutters on the windows.

The central building, called the Gedong Karangasem after its architectural style, contains Neolithic material. On the veranda are a handsome throne and a number of stone figures. As originally built by the Dutch, the gedong was open on all four sides; the walls were added later. The third building, in the style of the Tabanan palace, is richly decorated. On a platform in the centre of the hall are a number of Barong figures. Note the intricately carved roof beams.

Between the buildings is the "shower room" of the princely family; partly sunk into the ground, it may be overlooked at first glance.

★★Pura Jagat Natha

Immediately to the right of the main exit from the National Museum is the Pura Jagat Natha (Temple of the Rulers of the Worlds), dedicated to Sangyang Widi, who to the Balinese Hindus is the incarnation of Vishnu, the supreme god, and thus the "god of gods". The symbols of divinities in the temple (Sangyang Widi represented as a gleaming gold figure seated on a seven-tiered throne of coralline limestone) are venerated not merely by particular groups of the population but by all Balinese Hindus.

Some 550 m (600 yds) north-east of the National Museum can be found ★**St Joseph's Church** (R.C.), in which Christian beliefs are represented in characteristic Balinese style.

★Pura Maospahit

Irregular opening times
Plan p. 104

The Pura Maospahit is one of the most important temples in Denpasar and one of the oldest. There is reliable evidence that it dates from the 15th century.

As the name indicates, the temple was founded by the Majapahit dynasty (originally from Java), whose ancestral temple it still is. In the course of its history it has been frequently altered and embellished, and much of the original furnishings has been lost.

The main entrance to the temple, on Jalan Dr Sutomo, is opened only on days of festival; the normal entrance is on the left-hand side – though even

In the Bali National Museum ▶

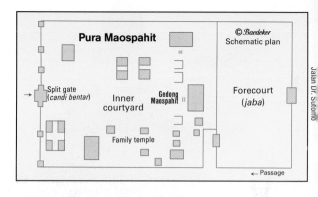

Jalan Dr. Sutomo

Schematic plan

Pura Maospahit

Split gate (*candi bentar*)

Inner courtyard

Gedong Maospahit

Family temple

Forecourt (*jaba*)

← Passage

this is not always open. To reach it, go along the narrow lane, Gang III, where with luck you may find an open door. There is another entrance leading directly into the main part of the temple, reached by continuing to the end of Gang III and turning right along the enclosure wall.

The temple is in two parts, separated from one another by a high wall. It is entered through a split gate (*candi bentar*), which is the most striking feature of the temple. On the five pillars of the gate are figures (from left to right) of the god Sangkara (a manifestation of Shiva), Indra (the sky god of ancient India), Yama (god of the dead), Bayu (god of the wind), Garuda (the bird which was Vishnu's mount), the Indian god Kubera (god of wealth) and the sea god Waruna.

To the right of the temple courtyard are a number of buildings which belong not to the Pura Maospahit but to a family temple. At the far end of the courtyard is the Gedong Maospahit, a shrine for the veneration of ancestors. To the left of this is a closed building dedicated to the worship of the ancestors of the Majapahit dynasty of eastern Java.

Particularly notable are three shrines for divinities (*pelinggih*) decorated with stags' antlers (a prerogative of the ancestors of the Majapahit dynasty).

★Werdi Budaya Art Centre

Werdi Budaya Art Centre (Jalan Bayusuta) is worth visiting both for the permanent exhibition of Balinese paintings in the main building and for the exhibition of work by both young and established artists for sale.

Behind the building is a luxuriant tropical garden with a number of small pools. There is also a large open-air theatre in which performances of Balinese dances are given during the annual Festival of Arts and occasionally at other times.

In a small building on the street leading to the Art Centre is a display of work by the German painter **Walter Spies** (see Famous People).

★Academy of Indonesian Dance

Near the Art Centre (Jalan Ratza) is the Academy of Indonesian Dance (Akademi Seni Tari Indonesia, ASTI), in which young Balinese are taught the high art of the traditional dances, the shadow play (wayang kulit) and the playing of the instruments of the gamelan orchestra. In the morning visitors can watch the pupils rehearsing, and in the evening there are performances in which they can demonstrate their skills. (For information about times of performances apply to the Bali Tourist Office in Denpasar: see Practical Information, Information.)

★★Pasar Badung

Daily 6am–4pm

In the angle between Jalan Gajah Mada (one of Denpasar's main traffic arteries) and Jalan Sulawesi is the town's largest market, the Pasar Badung, housed in a three-storey building. Fresh vegetables and fruit are sold in the basement, handicrafts, textiles, clothing, etc., on the upper floors. The Pasar Badung has its own domestic temple. Round the

Pasar Badung market centre

corner are the fishmongers – half concealed because the Balinese Hindus believe that the sea is inhabited by demons and evil spirits, as no doubt are the creatures that live in it.

Surroundings

Kuta, which has now become almost part of Denpasar and has joined up with Legian, once a separate little township, is now a typical tourist resort, vibrant with life until late at night and practically indistinguishable from any other busy resort. The inhabitants of these one-time fishing villages have long hung up their nets and now earn their living from tourism.

Kuta, Legian

The centre of activity in Kuta is Jalan Legian, which is lined with restaurants, bars and shops, as well as a number of rather more dubious establishments. Those who do their shopping here and pay the almost invariably steep prices have only themselves to blame. Food and drink are much cheaper elsewhere; but, evening after evening, the atmosphere of Kuta and Legian draws crowds of visitors, anxious to see and be seen.

The beach of Kuta is hardly a "tropical dream beach", being separated from the hotels and restaurants by a busy road. Legian's beach is rather quieter, and is the one favoured by the trend-setters of the day.

Padang Galak is only a few kilometres east of Denpasar and is easily reached by bus, bemo or hired car.

Padang Galak

Padang Galak attracts large numbers of local people and visitors to its annual **Kite Festival**, held on a weekend in July. The original object of this event was to give a boost to the Balinese craft of kite-making, but it has also developed into a major tourist attraction.

Sanur

Much quieter than Kuta and Legian is the resort of Sanur, south-east of Denpasar, even though this too has been enjoying something of a boom in recent years. Its development began in 1967 with the building of the first hotel of international standard, the Bali Beach Hotel. This high-rise concrete structure aroused local opposition and led to a ban on the erection of buildings higher than the tallest palm-tree in the area.

Sanur is regarded as a more select resort than Kuta or Legian, and the beach is lined by luxury hotels. Perhaps for this reason, the sand is also rather cleaner.

Near the Bali Beach Hotel is the **Le Mayeur House**, built by the Belgian painter of that name (d. 1958), which contains a collection of his work. Open daily 10am–2pm; there is a small admission charge.

Lembongan

The island of Lembongan (see Penida) can be reached from Sanur by outboard or motor boat; the crossing takes about an hour.

Gianyar   M 7

Region: Central Bali
District: Gianyar
Altitude: 127 m (417 ft)

Access

By road: from Denpasar north-east to Sakah; then turn right for Blahbatuh and Gianyar.
Bus: several times daily from Denpasar-Kereneng.
Bemo: along road.

Gianyar, in the 17th and 18th century the capital of a powerful kingdom and now chief town of Gianyar district, lies 26 km (16 mi.) north-east of Denpasar in a well watered and intensively cultivated upland region, mainly devoted to rice-growing. It has a modest textile industry which makes a contribution to the economy of the region.

History As Gianyar's near neighbour Klungkung, capital of the most powerful kingdom on Bali from the 15th to the 17th century, declined, so the authority of the Rajas of Gianyar increased. During the period of Dutch occupation they reached an accommodation with the invaders, and as a result Gianyar was spared intervention by the colonial authorities and the ruling family retained their influence.

Sights

Little is left of the former splendour of the princely capital. The townscape is now dominated by modern functional buildings.

★★Puri Gianyar

Admission only
with permission

The palace of Puri Gianyar, built in 1771 by Dewa Manggis IV, lies on one side of the village's central square. It is normally not open to the public; but if you are lucky a member of the princely family, who still occupy the palace, may be prepared to let you in.

The palace consists of a number of pavilions in traditional Balinese style, with magnificent woodcarving. Also notable, in addition to the carving in the interior of the palace, are the figures in the charming tropical garden.

Surroundings

★Blahbatuh

5 km (3 mi.) south-west of Gianyar lies the quiet little market township of Blahbatuh, which has two notable temples.

In the palace of the Rajas of Gianyar

On the Denpasar road is the Pura Dalem Blahbatuh, with a seated figure of Buddha amid Hindu figures – evidence, perhaps, of the tolerance of the Balinese in religious matters.

The other temple is the Pura Puseh Blahbatuh or Pura Gaduh, rebuilt after its almost complete destruction in an earthquake in 1917. It contains a colossal head of a giant, said by the local people to be Jero Gede Mecaling, who according to legend came to Bali several times from the island of Penida (see entry) and wrought great mischief with his demons and devils.

Gilimanuk   B 3

Region: West Bali
District: Jembrana
Altitude: sea level

By road: 130 km (80 mi.) north-west of Denpasar on a road which skirts the coast for much of the way.
Bus and bemo: regular services daily from Denpasar-Ubung.

Access

Gilimanuk, the most westerly town on Bali, lies on the Bali Strait, only 2.5 km (1½ mi.) wide, between Bali and Java. It is important as a ferry and commercial port providing a link with the larger neighbouring island.

Gilimanuk must be the town on Bali with the fewest tourist sights. Visitors may be interested to watch the busy activity around the harbour, centred mainly on the ferry traffic, or to visit the market held every evening in the town centre, with some good hot food stalls.

A few kilometres before Gilimanuk on the road from Denpasar interesting **detours** can be made to the little village of Palasari (with Roman Catholic inhabitants) and to Blimbingsari, most of whose inhabitants are Protestants.

There are regular **ferry** services from Gilimanuk to Ketapang on the neighbouring island of Java (at the end of the main street bear left and follow the signposts). Places can be booked and tickets bought in the harbour. The crossing takes about 30 to 45 minutes.

Goa Gajah (Elephant Cave)

See Bedulu

Goa Lawah (Bat Cave)

See Candi Dasa, Surroundings

Gunung (5 hill, mountain)

Gunung Abang: see Penelokan, Surroundings
Gunung Agung: see Besakih, Surroundings
Gunung Batukau: see Tabanan, Surroundings
Gunung Batur: see Penelokan, Surroundings
Gunung Kawi: see Tampaksiring, Surroundings
Gunung Rinjani: see Lombok

Kapal   L 7

Region: South-West Bali
District: Badung
Altitude: 75 m (245 ft)

Access

By road: from Denpasar north on Singaraja road.
Bus: good services from Denpasar-Ubung.
Bemo: regular services from Denpasar and Mengwi.

The little town of Kapal lies 15 km (9 mi.) north-west of Denpasar, a few

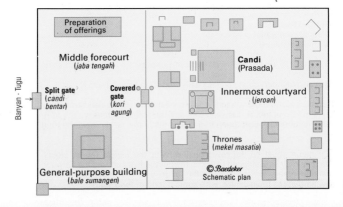

Outer forecourt (jaba sisi)

Preparation of offerings

Middle forecourt (jaba tengah)

Candi (Prasada)

Banyan · Tugu

Split gate (candi bentar)

Covered gate (kori agung)

Innermost courtyard (jeroan)

Thrones (mekel masatia)

General-purpose building (bale sumangen)

© Baedeker
Schematic plan

kilometres before Mengwi. It is famed for the excellent quality of its sculpture and other products made of cement and stone, and many temple figures and other objects made of these materials come from here. Although these are attractive examples of local craftsmanship they are also heavy, and before buying any of them visitors will want to consider the high cost of shipping them home.

Sights

Along the main road are numbers of shops open to the street in which stone figures, house temples, etc. are displayed and also offered for sale. In view of the usually heavy weight, before purchasing these otherwise quite charming and well made articles, the problem of expensive transport must be taken into consideration.

The Pura Sada (Prasada) is one of the most important temples on Bali, founded by the Rajas of Mengwi, whose ancestors came from Klungkung. It can be reached only on foot (15 minutes' walk; follow the main road to Kapanan, then turn left into a narrow lane).

★★ Pura Sada

The present buildings stand on the foundations of an earlier temple, probably of the 12th century.
  The temple appears at first to consist of only two parts, since the outer forecourt, with a large *waringin* tree, is not enclosed by walls. The middle forecourt is entered by a seven-tiered split gate (*candi korung*), probably dating from the 14th or 15th century.
  In the inner courtyard, to the left, is the *bale pesamyangan*, in which the gods were welcomed to the temple. Beyond this is a massive *prasada* in Majapahit style, rebuilt in 1948–49 after the destruction of its predecessor (which probably also dated from the 14th or 15th century) in the devastating earthquake of 1917. It is not certain, however, that it stands on its original site. Particularly notable is a grotesquely grimacing demon in the upper part of the pagoda.
  In the centre of the courtyard is a pond (now empty), symbolising the abode of the celestial nymph Widadari, a mediator between the world of the gods and the world of men. To the right of this are 57 stone thrones for the ancestors of the Mengwi dynasty, and on the east side are three larger thrones.
  To the rear of the courtyard can be seen a number of shrines and thrones, dedicated to the divine trinity of Brahma, Vishnu and Shiva and to other divinities.

This very interesting village temple stands directly on the main road through Kapal. There are actually two temples, the Pura Desa and **Pura Puseh**, but they are built so closely together that their original separateness can be detected only by the initiated.
The richly decorated gate has three entrances, one for each member of the divine trinity. To right and left of the gate are finely carved reliefs depicting scenes from Tantric animal fables.

★★ Pura Desa

Surroundings

The two small villages of Sempidi and Lukluk, a few kilometres before Kapal on the road from Denpasar, have fine **village temples** with a profusion of decoration on their gates and walls.

Karangasem

See Amlapura

Kintamani

See Penelokan, Surroundings

Klungkung   N 7

Region: East Bali
District: KlungKung
Altitude: up to 160 m (525 ft)
Population: 17,000

By road: from Denpasar east via Gianyar.   Access
Bus: good regular services from Denpasar-Kereneng.
Bemo: from Denpasar.

Klungkung, once capital of a powerful kingdom, lies at the foot of a region of gently undulating hills, with the volcano of Gunung Agung forming an impressive backdrop in clear weather. It is now a busy medium-sized town forming an important link between central Bali and the eastern part of the island, which after the devastating eruption of 1963 and the accompanying earthquakes was cut off both physically and economically from the rest of the island for some considerable time.

History Among the Hindus from Java who sought refuge on Bali towards the end of the 15th century to escape persecution was Batu Renggong, son of Prince Widjaya. In order to escape imprisonment his father had burned himself alive – a fate which his son did not wish to share. With a few hundred followers, including many priests, he fled to Bali and built a palace at Gelgel, a little town 5 km (3 mi.) south of Klungkung, assuming the style of Dewa Agung (Grand Prince) and declaring Gelgel his capital.

About 1710 the royal court moved to the more conveniently situated town of Klungkung, where Prince Di Made, a great-grandson of Widjaya, built a new palace. The town's principal sight, the Kerta Gosa (Court Hall), probably also dates from this period. Thereafter Klungkung grew steadily in importance, to such an extent that all important legal disputes from anywhere on Bali were dealt with, and criminals from all over the island were tried, in the Court Hall in Klungkung.

Klungkung also played an important part during the Dutch attempts to occupy Bali. After the Dutch landing in the north of Bali and their capture of Singaraja, Buleleng and other towns, an advance party led by Captain Cornelis de Houtman reached Klungkung, where they were welcomed as guests by the Dewa Agung, who was much interested in the European way of life. Soon afterwards it was agreed to establish trading relations.

During the 18th century Klungkung increasingly lost importance and influence to nearby Gianyar. The Dewa Agung reached agreement with the neighbouring princedoms on common action against the Dutch, but he lacked the military means to resist the threatened invasion; and so, after Buleleng to the north and Amlapura to the east, Klungkung became one of the first territories to be conquered by the Dutch.

Then in 1908 occurred an event which still arouses strong emotions among the Balinese. Dutch troops occupied Klungkung and took up position before the gates of the palace, whereupon the gates opened and a procession of 250 men, women and children, led by the Dewa Agung emerged, advanced towards the invaders and halted. The Dewa Agung drew his kris and plunged it in his heart; his example was followed by

◀ *Split gate* (candi bentar): a *symbol of the divided Mount Meru* his retinue, and those who survived were killed by Dutch bullets. (Note the similar event at Denpasar.)

Sights

Little is left of the one-time splendour of Klungkung, for after the conquest the Dutch pulled down almost all the major buildings. In recent years a few old buildings have been restored or reconstructed, but the pattern of present-day Klungkung is set by modern functional buildings. Only during the 1980s were some of the buildings repaired or reconstructed. They recall the town's heyday when Klungkung was the artistic and cultural centre of Bali and produced numerous important painters.

In the centre of town is the **Taman Gili** (= garden of the island), a well-kept park which has roughly the same outlines as the Puri Agung, the princely residence of former times. In the middle of a lake covered with lotus flowers stands the Bale Kembang, a small pavilion with beautiful Wayang paintings inside.

★★Kerta Gosa

Of the old palace of Puri Agung, which stood on the main street leading to the town centre, only two structures remain – an entrance gate, now standing by itself, and the Kerta Gosa (Court Hall). They stand opposite one another in an attractive park, roughly of the same extent as the former palace precinct.

The Kerta Gosa, built in the mid 18th century on a small island in an artificial pond, is particularly notable for its magnificent ceiling paintings in the *wayang* style.

Originally the paintings were on canvas, but in the course of restoration work in 1960 they were transferred to fibrous cement sheets. Paintings in the *wayang* style (in which some artists in and around

Ceiling paintings in the Kerta Gosa (Court Hall)

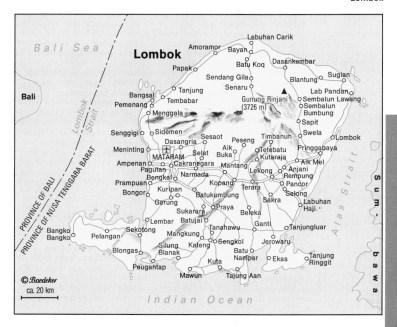

chains are already putting out feelers, and a Sheraton Hotel is to be built on the south coast of Lombok by 1995.

Nevertheless it will be some years before Lombok goes the same way as Bali. Until then visitors should be careful to take account of the special circumstances of Lombok. The inhabitants have not had the experience of tourism to anything like the same extent as the people of Bali, and things that are accepted or tolerated to a greater or lesser degree on Bali may give offence on Lombok. This should be borne in mind particularly by visitors who find their way into the interior of the island and come into contact with the Sasaks, the indigenous inhabitants of Lombok.

Size With an area of 4692 sq. km (1812 sq. mi.), Lombok is only slightly smaller than Bali. The two islands are separated by the Lombok Strait (Selat Lombok), 40 km (25 mi.) wide and up to 3000 m (10,000 ft) deep, which also marks the boundary (the Wallace Line) between Malayo-Asian and Malayo-Australian flora and fauna.

The highest point on the island is the volcano of Gunung Rinjani (3726 m (12,225 ft)), the third highest peak in Indonesia. Extending from east to west, Mt Rinjani and its foothills occupy almost the whole of the northern half of the island.

Access Lombok can be reached from Bali by air (Merpati airline, a subsidiary of Garuda) in half an hour, by speedboat in 2½ hours and by car ferry in 4½ hours. There are several services daily by all three means of transport. Lombok's airport is a few kilometres north of Mataram. Speedboats and ferries sail between Padang Bai on Bali and Lembar, 30 km (19 mi.) south-west of Mataram.

The central bemo station is 7 km (4½ mi.) from Ampenan and 2.5 km (1½ mi.) from Cakranegara.

History Ruled in the 17th century by Balinese princes of the Karangasem dynasty (who regarded it merely as an appendage to their kingdom), Lombok was occupied in the first half of the 18th century by the rulers of the island of Sulawesi (Celebes). In 1740, however, the western part of the island was recovered by the Karangasem dynasty, who then controlled eastern Bali (see Amlapura).

The eastern part of Lombok continued to be ruled by the Muslim princes of southern Sulawesi until 1849, when the Raja of Karangasem incorporated the whole island in his kingdom. In 1838 the united princedom of Lombok was established, and five years later the Raja of Mataram recognised Dutch sovereignty. In 1891 the Dutch crushed a rising by the Sasaks and then incorporated the whole of Lombok in the Dutch East Indies. Thereafter Lombok was a convenient base from which to launch punitive expeditions against Bali. The Sasak rulers of Lombok were very ready to support such actions, since they saw the Dutch forces as enabling them to shake off the hegemony of Bali.

Lombok is now part of the Indonesian province of Nusa Tenggara Barat.

Lombok has a **population** of some 2.4 million, 80 per cent of whom are Sasaks, the original inhabitants of the island. Although Bali is only 40 km (25 mi.) away, there are no more than about 80,000 Balinese on Lombok. Both islands were settled at about the same time, probably by members of the same tribe from southern China. In the 17th century there was a further influx of Chinese to work in the rice-fields.

The Sasaks are believed to have originally come from north-western India, and possibly also from Burma, from where they migrated

Children in a Sasak village

about the 14th century. Evidence of their Burmese origin may be the similarity of Sasak costumes with those of the hill tribes of Burma.

The Sasaks live mainly by farming. As on Bali, rice-growing plays a major part in the economy, though the rice terraces of Lombok are much less elaborately and systematically laid out than the rice-fields of Bali. There are also vegetable and tobacco plantations, the produce of which serves mainly to meet the needs of the local population; little of it is exported.

Although in recent decades there has been a trend towards urbanisation on Lombok, the great majority of the Sasaks still live in their typical **villages**. The characteristic features of these villages built in traditional style are the "rice-houses" (*lumbung*). Usually square in shape and constructed exclusively of natural materials (clay and wood), these are raised on stilts and roofed with grass or sometimes rice straw. The *lumbung* is a very practical building: on ground level are the domestic and working animals, in the middle is the accommodation for the family, and under the high, curved roof are stored supplies of provisions.

Sasak houses are now being imitated in the construction of new hotels.

Religion In contrast to the Balinese, the great majority of the people of Lombok were converted to Islam in the 16th century, and with the exception of a tiny Hindu minority, mainly in the west of the island, they are still Muslims – though there are still believers, particularly in the mountain villages in the north of the island, in the old Wetu Telu religion, which shows features of the cult of ancestors, Islam and Hinduism as well as the veneration of natural shrines.

Sights

Mataram

Mataram is the chief town of Lombok and the administrative centre of the Indonesian province of Nusa Tenggara Barat. It is now for all practical purposes amalgamated with the two formerly independent townships of Ampenan and Cakranegara, but each has preserved something of its distinctive character.

Mataram itself is a kind of garden city, in which all the main agencies of the provincial government have their offices.

Apart from the Museum there are no features of tourist interest in the area, unless the busy and colourful life of the town is so regarded. There are, however, a number of places to see within easy reach of the town.

A visit to the ★**Museum of Mataram** (Jalan Panji Tilarnegara) is essential for anyone interested in the history of Lombok, and particularly in the history of its people. In addition to various documents and written material the exhibits include numerous tools and implements, utensils, weapons and local craft products. The structure of the traditional Sasak houses is illustrated by lovingly constructed models. Most of the items have labels in Indonesian and English.

Open Sun.–Thu. 8am–2pm, Fri. 8–11am

The ★**Meru Temple** was built in 1720 by the Balinese Prince Karang. In the innermost precinct of the extensive complex are several *merus* dedicated to the Hindu trinity of Shiva, Vishnu and Brahma.

Ampenan, situated directly on the sea, is still a port town, though it has

Ampenan

Lombok

The beaches of Lombok are still largely unspoiled

Fishing boats on the beach

Fishermen with their catch

Entrance to the Hindu shrine in the Lingsar Temple

lost much of its earlier importance. Near Ampenan is Lombok's only airport.

In the colourful markets and bazaars of Cakranegara the pattern is set by the Chinese who have come to settle on Lombok over the centuries. The local people refer to it mockingly as Chinatown.

Cakranegara

The Lingsar Temple, at the village of Narmada (a short distance north of Cakranegara), is venerated both by Hindus and by adherents of the Wetu Telu religion. The temple attracts large numbers of pilgrims of both faiths on a particular day at the beginning of the rainy season (October–December).
    A split gate (*candi bentar*) leads into a broad avenue with a pool on either side. Half way along, on the left, is a Hindu temple on a square base (no admittance), with four shrines; the one on the left is oriented on Gunung Agung, the abode of the gods on the neighbouring island of Bali.
    There is a separate temple for those of the Wetu Telu faith. Beyond this are pools in which worshippers perform ritual ablutions.

★**Lingsar Temple**

Near Jalan Selaparang is the Mayura Water Palace, built about 1744, which was part of the palace of the Princes of Bali. This is a hall, open on all four sides, situated in an artificial lake and reached on a narrow causeway. It was used both as a court hall and for meetings of the Hindu princes.

**Mayura
Water Palace**

Along the shore to the north of Ampenan is the Water Temple of Pura Segara. The road to it runs through a number of small fishing villages with brightly painted boats.
    Near the Pura Segara are a Chinese and a Muslim cemetery.

Pura Segara

Mayura Water Palace ...   *... and its bell-tower (kulkul)*

Senggigi

18 km (11 mi.) north of Ampenan, in an area where only a few years ago
the local children played undisturbed on the beach, is the new tourist
centre of Senggigi Beach, with a number of reasonable hotels, restaurants and bars. The only attractions are the bathing and the various
activities on the beach, where the holidaymakers are assailed, particularly in the evening, by hawkers selling refreshments and a variety of
wares.

Sukarara

The little settlement of Sukarara, 25 km (15 mi.) south-east of Mataram,
is famed for the hand-woven fabrics in traditional style made by the villagers. These fine textiles, which often involve months of work, are sold
in the village at prices which reflect their quality.

★★Gunung Rinjani

The ascent of the volcano of Gunung Rinjani, the third highest mountain
in the Indonesian archipelago, is one of the great experiences of a visit
to Lombok. But the climb should not be undertaken with any idea of setting new records: plenty of time should be allowed for enjoying the
beauty of this volcanic landscape, which was declared a nature reserve
in 1984.

Gunung Rinjani (3726 m (12,225 ft)), which is revered both by Sasaks
and by Balinese as a sacred mountain, can be climbed by a number of

different routes. The route recommended here is the relatively easy ascent from Senaru on the north side of the mountain. Here you will find local guides offering their services and, almost certainly, other visitors who will be glad to make up a group. The guide can be expected to provide or obtain the necessary equipment.

From Mataram a bus or bemo can be taken to Anyar, from which it is only a few kilometres to Senaru. The best plan is to spend the night there and set out on the following morning on the 12 km (7½ mi.) climb to the crater lake of Segara Anak. This part of the ascent gives no difficulty: it is a matter mainly of following a well trodden track and waymarks numbered from 1 to 200.

The climb from Segara Anak to the summit calls for physical fitness as well as plenty of time (around 4½ hours). From the summit there are superb views of the crater lake and the whole of Lombok, and also of Bali's sacred mountain, Gunung Agung.

Outside the rainy season the descent from the summit to the crater lake, with the necessary care, takes a good 3 hours. From the lake there is a path (1½ hours) to the hot springs (up to 70°C (158°F), with a high sulphur content) where the little river Kali Putih ("White River") rises. Here and on the shores of the crater lake are simple camping sites which make it possible to extend the expedition to several days.

★ Gili Islands

The three small islands Gili Air, Gili Meno and Gili Trawangan lie only a few miles off the north-west coast of Lombok. They can be reached by boat from the harbour of the little town of Pemenang; the crossing takes from 20 minutes to one hour.

Sights The Gilis – as they have been known for a long time by watersport enthusiasts from all over the world – offer beautiful beaches and an underwater world which is almost intact. Any type of motor traffic is forbidden, the traditional cidomos (pony carriages) are used for transport. Most accommodation offers only modest comfort but it is good value for money. The best places for diving and snorkelling are found on Gili Trawangan which at 300 hectares is the largest island of the Gilis. The equipment can be hired. The Oberoi hotel on Lombok is a good starting point for excursions to the Gilis.

Mengwi   L 7

Region: South-West Bali
District: Badung. Altitude: 95 m (310 ft)

By road: from Denpasar north on the Singaraja road.   Access
Bus: regular services from Denpasar–Ubung.
Bemo: along road or from Denpasar–Ubung bemo station.
The town of Mengwi lies 16 km (10 mi.) north-west of Denpasar.

History Mengwi was once capital of the princedom of that name, whose rulers repeatedly contrived to reach an accommodation with other powers. They achieved this not only in their conflicts with the princes of Klungkung and Gianyar but also, at a later stage, during the period of Dutch colonial rule, in which the Rajas of Mengwi rapidly acquiesced.

In 1891 the rulers of Tabanan and Badung conquered the princedom of Mengwi, divided it between them and thus put an end to its independence.

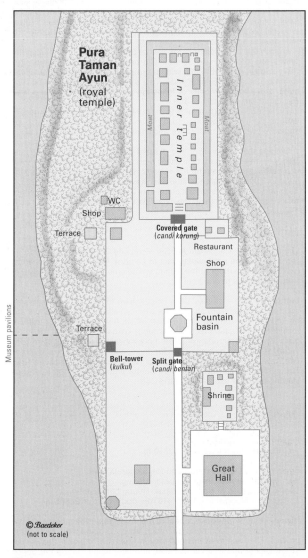

**Pura
Taman
Ayun**
(royal
temple)

Inner Temple

Moat

Moat

WC

Shop

Terrace

Covered gate
(*candi korung*)

Restaurant

Shop

Fountain
basin

Museum pavilions

Terrace

Bell-tower
(*kulkul*)

Split gate
(*candi bentar*)

Shrine

Great
Hall

© *Baedeker*
(not to scale)

Sights

★★Pura Taman
Ayun

The Pura Taman Ayun ("Garden Temple in the Water") is one of the six (according to an unofficial count) royal temples on Bali, and thus one of the most important temples on the island. This imposing complex stands on an island in a river, and the inner temple is in addition sur-

Pura Taman Ayun: pagoda and ...

... throne for the gods

rounded by a moat. In front of the entrance to the inner temple, beyond a split gate (*candi bentar*), is a large fountain basin dedicated to the rulers of the underworld.

In the innermost courtyard, which is entered through a covered gate (*candi korung*), are no fewer than 27 buildings of varying size and function.

The Pura Taman Ayun is one of the network of temples which covers Bali. Its importance can be judged from the fact that in this temple are venerated not only the divinities for whom it was built but also those who visit it on the occasion of festivals. Among them are the gods who dwell on Gunung Agung and Gunung Batur. An eleven-tiered *meru* (at the far end, in the right-hand corner) is dedicated to the rice goddess Dewi Sri. The third bale on the left is believed to be the abode of several different gods.

The Pura Taman Ayun was built in 1637, in the reign of Raja Gusti Agung Anom. It was given its present form about 1937, when it was considerably enlarged.

Visitors are ferried on a raft to two **museum** pavilions with pictures and models illustrating the Manusia Yadnya ceremonies.

Surroundings

Like so much on Bali, the monkey forest of Sangeh (20 km (13 mi.) from Denpasar, 10 km (6 mi.) from Mengwi) has been taken over by the tourist trade. Before reaching the forest in which hundreds of monkeys live in natural conditions, visitors must run the gauntlet of the souvenir shops which line the path from the car park. It goes without saying that both

★Sangeh

the souvenirs and the peanuts which are fed to the monkeys are dearer here than elsewhere.

According to legend the monkeys are descended from the monkey king Hanuman and are therefore sacred. They are venerated in the Pura Bukit Sari, a temple in the forest which probably dates from the 17th century. More impressive than the temple, however, are the mighty trees of the forest. It is not known where they came from, for they are of a species not normally found on Bali.

Warning The monkeys, particularly females with young, are sometimes fairly aggressive. When walking in the forest you should keep cameras and handbags firmly closed; and spectacle-wearers should be particularly wary, since the monkeys are fond of snatching visitors' glasses.

Marga

15 km (9 mi.) north-north-west of Mengwi is Marga, with the Marga National Memorial, commemorating a battle with Dutch forces on November 20th 1946. There is a cemetery with the graves of 1371 Balinese who fell in the battle, and nearby a memorial museum.

Negara   D 5

Region: West Bali
District: Jembrana
Altitude: 120 m (395 ft)

Access

By road: 97 km (60 mi.) from Denpasar in direction of Gilimanuk.
Bus: regular services from Denpasar–Tegal.
Bemo: from Denpasar not advisable; better from Gilimanuk or Pulukan.

Negara, situated in one of the most thinly populated parts of Bali, is the Balinese town with the largest Muslim population – the result of its nearness to the neighbouring, predominantly Muslim, island of Java. Apart from its status as chief town of Jembrana district Negara has no particular claims to the tourist's attention.

Sights

Negara itself has no particular tourist attractions, but it is a trim little town with a number of handsome houses typical of the local style of building.

There are a number of mosques, which visitors can enter outside the hours of prayer; permission should, however, be asked before entering.

★★**Water-buffalo races** There is one annual event which brings a little life to this otherwise sleepy little town – the water-buffalo races which have been held here for the last hundred years or so in November and attract thousands of visitors, for many of whom the betting is an additional attraction. The exact date varies from year to year: ask at your hotel reception or a tourist office in Denpasar for information.

The race is run by two-wheeled carts drawn by a pair of buffaloes, which are controlled by a "jockey" whose task is, on the one hand, to keep his balance and, on the other, to urge the rather clumsy beasts to greater speed. The astonishing fact is that they manage to achieve speeds of up to 50 km (30 mi.) an hour over the 2.5 km (1½ mi.) long course.

Surroundings

Pulukan

The road from Denpasar to Negara runs through the little town of

Pulukan, which may attract visitors who want to get away from the throngs of tourists. The accommodation available offers only a modest standard of comfort, but the beaches are ideal for surfing.

See Gilimanuk

See Gilimanuk

Nusa Dua

See Bukit Badung Peninsula

Nusa Lembongan

See Penida, Lembongan

Nusa Penida

See Penida

Padang Bai

See Candi Dasa, Surroundings

Padang Galak

See Denpasar, Surroundings

Pecatu

See Bukit Badung Peninsula

Pejeng

See Bedulu, Surroundings

Peliatan   M 7

Region: Central Bali
District: Gianyar
Altitude: 66 m (217 ft)

By road: from Denpasar north-east on the Ubud road. Peliatan is a few kilometres before Ubud.
Bus and bemo: regular services from Denpasar-Kereneng and from Ubud.

Access

The village of Peliatan, half way between Ubud and Mas, is favoured by visitors who want a quiet country holiday, well away from the bustle of the tourist centres. It has a number of hotels in different categories, and

in the last few years one or two with a high standard of amenity have been opened.

Two of the best known Balinese dance groups are based in Peliatan, and their rehearsals, in the former princely palace of Puri Agung, are sometimes open to the public (information in Ubud).

Sights

Peliatan is not a particularly interesting village, and its temples are not of particular importance, with one exception – Pura Pande, the Temple of the Smiths. It is a reminder that on Bali each professional group has its own temple, dedicated to the gods who offer its members protection and counsel.

★Pura Pande

The Pura Pande has a very handsome covered gate (*candi korung*) built of red brick and white tufa. On the protective wall (*aling-aling*) beyond the gate designed to keep out demons is a fine Garuda figure. There is another *aling-aling* in front of the steps leading up to the innermost precinct of the temple.

The picture gallery of Agung Rai is the largest of its kind on Bali.

★★Agung Rai

Agung Rai, a scion of a princely family, has been for many years a committed collector and patron of Balinese art. He has given many Balinese artists the opportunity of showing their work to a wider public and making a livelihood by selling them; and he invests the profit from works sold in the showroom attached to the gallery in the purchase of further works, thus building up his collection to its present considerable size.

Open daily
8am–5pm

Admission charge

Penelokan   N 4

Region: North Bali
District: Bangli
Altitude: 1452 m (4764 ft)

By road: from Denpasar No. 27 to Bedulu, then No. 31 to Lake Batur.
Bus: several services daily from Denpasar–Kereneng.
Bemo: from Denpasar and along road.

Access

The name Penelokan means "beautiful view", and this is certainly no misnomer. From this little hill village there are breathtaking views of a fascinating landscape dominated by the volcano (quiescent since 1963) of Gunung Batur and its crater lake.

Penelokan, like the nearby village of Batur (see below), formerly lay immediately below the volcano. The villagers stoically accepted the damage caused by eruptions in 1917 and 1926, but after the major eruption of 1963 (which took place at about the same time as the eruption of Gunung Agung) they resolved to rebuild their village on a safer site on the rim of the crater.

Sights

Apart from the magnificent view of Gunung Batur and Lake Batur (illustration, p. 12) Penelokan has no features of particular interest. Such sights as it had were destroyed in the most recent eruptions of the volcano. Among them was a temple containing a shrine dedicated to the goddess Dewi Danu, who is much revered as protective goddess of the water of Lake Batur. As if by a miracle the shrine was spared by the flows of lava and is now in the Pura Ulun Danu Batur (see below).

◀ *Covered gate (*candi korung*) in the Pura Pande, Peliatan*

Surroundings

★★Gunung Abang

Penelokan is a good base from which to undertake the 4-hour climb to the summit of the volcano of Gunung Abang. At 2153 m (7064 ft), it is fully 400 m (1300 ft) higher than Gunung Batur, on the opposite side of Lake Batur, which can also be climbed from Penelokan.

★★Lake Batur

With an area of about 140 sq. km (54 sq. mi.), the crater of Gunung Batur is one of the largest volcanic craters in the world. It was formed millions of years ago by the collapse of a chamber containing volcanic magma which had been partly emptied by an eruption. In the centre of the caldera is Lake Batur, which is now up to 100 m (330 ft) deep.

★★Gunung Batur

The ascent of Gunung Batur (also known as Gunung Lebah, the "Mountain in the Depths") is a great scenic experience, and is not too difficult a climb: the summit can be reached, even by less experienced climbers, in about three hours. Stout footwear is essential for walking on the loose lava rubble and scree. Since the hill is frequently shrouded in dense cloud even in the morning, an early start is advisable.

Leave Penelokan on the road which runs down to Kedisan, and at the village of Toya Bungkah on the west side of Lake Batur, which is noted for its hot sulphur springs, take a well waymarked path which runs up Gunung Batur through magnificent scenery. It is important not to leave the path, since there may be danger from fumaroles. From the summit there are superb views of the barren landscape with its bizarre lava formations, the valley below and Gunung Abang on the opposite side of the crater.

Great care is necessary in walking round Gunung Batur. A good head for heights is essential, since at some points there are arêtes with deep abysses on both sides.

Gunung Batur can also be climbed in about three hours from the village of Pura Yati.

Kintamani

6 km (4 mi.) north-west of Penelokan on road No. 35, shortly before the lively market village of Kintamani, which straggles along the road, is the village of Batur, with the temple of Pura Ulun Danu Batur.

★Batur

The temple buildings are grouped round a shrine dedicated to Dewi Danu, goddess of lakes and rivers, in the form of an eleven-tiered **meru**, which survived the eruptions of 1926 and 1963. There are a number of other *merus*, which form an impressive backdrop, particularly in the morning and evening.

The temple complex, built of black lava, has been constantly extended over the years, and when finally complete will comprise almost 300 buildings. Note particularly the demons round the entrance, guardians and protectors against evil spirits.

The village of Batur was threatened by the eruption of 1917, and nine years later was partly destroyed by lava flows. The villagers then abandoned the old village and built a new one higher up, on a site which seemed to them safer. The move proved a wise one, for the village escaped the flow of lava in the 1963 eruption. It now offers reasonably priced accommodation for visitors.

★Pura Tegeh Koripan

5 km (3 mi.) north of Kintamani, on Mt Penulisan (1745 m (5725 ft)), stands the Pura Tegeh Koripan, the highest temple on Bali. It is reached on a path with over 400 steps – a climb to be undertaken only by visitors in sufficiently fit condition. The climb is best done in the early morning or late afternoon.

The temple, from which there are fine views of the surrounding country, dates from the 11th century and is thought to have been a royal temple of the Warmadewa dynasty of Pejeng. It is entered through two split gates. Before the entrance, on the left, is a cube-shaped stone with

Balinese children: interested and curious

a lingam preserved only in fragmentary form which is highly revered.

Within the temple are a number of *bales* containing stone figures, some of which are believed to date from the Javanese (Hindu) period on Bali. Particularly notable are figures of Vishnu and Lakshmi holding a four-petalled lotus blossom. There are also fine figures of Shiva, Parvati, Ganesha and a four-headed Brahma. In the centre of the courtyard is a throne which is occupied by Shiva, lord of the mountains, when he attends ceremonies in the temple.

In the past tourists were recommended not to visit the village of Trunyan, on the east side of Lake Batur, which is still occupied by a few Old Balinese (Bali Aga). The villagers have the reputation of being mistrustful of all strangers and of giving visitors a suspicious and sometimes downright unfriendly reception. More recently they appear to have recognised the (financial) advantages of tourism and to be less hostile to visitors. It is still the tradition in Trunyan, however, that any inhabitant of the village who marries a stranger must leave the village.

Trunyan

Penglipuran

See Bangli, Surroundings

Penida   O–Q 9/10

District: Klungkung. Area: 322 sq. km (124 sq. mi.)
Altitude: 0–529 m (0–1736 ft.) Population: 48,000

Penida

The island of Penida, with the two smaller islands of Ceningan and Lembongan off its north-west coast, lies off the south-east coast of Bali. The islanders are mainly Muslims. Across the island from north-west to south-east runs a range of limestone hills rising to a height of 529 m (1736 ft).

None of the islands has a very productive economy. The permeable karstic terrain is unsuitable for agriculture, and the inhabitants earn a modest living mainly from fishing. Formerly it was a place of exile for prisoners sentenced in Klungkung.

The Balinese, with their belief in spirits, are highly mistrustful of Penida. They believe it to be the abode of a particularly evil giant named Jero Gede Mecaling, who is said to have crossed the Badung Strait on several occasions with his train of spirits and brought terror and destruction to Bali, withdrawing only after the Balinese made a figure of another similar demon and set it up on the coast. And even today, when on New Year's eve (see Baedeker Special, p. 164) the Balinese carry huge demon figures through their villages and then take them down to the coast and burn them they still have in mind the terrifying giant Jero Gede Mecaling. The main attractions of Penida for visitors are the coasts, which offer ideal conditions for surfing and scuba diving.

Access Speedboats cross from Padang Bai (south-west of Amlapura) to Toyapakeh several times daily; the crossing takes about 40 minutes. Outboard motorboats sail daily (in the morning) from Kusamba (south-east of Klungkung) to Sampalan and Toyapakeh (about 2½ hours).

Sights

Sampalan

The chief place on Penida is Sampalan. The town has no sights of any interest, except the busy market which is held daily near the harbour.

Market in Sampalan: spices and ...   *... fish*

To the west of Sampalan, at the port village of Toyapakeh, can be seen the temple of Pura Ped, in a square artificial pond.

★Pura Ped

5 km (3 mi.) south-east of Sampalan the cave of Goa Karangasari contains an underground freshwater lake. The entrance to the cave system is not easy to find, being only 2.50 m (8 ft) across. It consists of a large and imposing chamber with a number of small caves opening off it. A powerful electric torch is essential; it can be hired from one of the locals who cluster outside the cave offering their services as guides. It is possible to continue through the cave system to another exit in a steep rock face.

★★Goa Karangasari

On the west coast of Penida are a number of beautiful bathing **beaches**; the beach at Toyapakeh in particular offers good bathing, snorkelling and scuba diving. Swimmers should remember that the tides are strong, that there are sometimes dangerous currents and that sharks are occasionally sighted here.

Bathing is not possible on the south coast of the island, where there are impressive **cliffs** up to 200 m (650 ft) high falling sheer down to the sea and lashed by fierce surf.

Lembongan

Access The little neighbouring island of Lembongan (landing-stage at Jungutbatu) can be reached from Penida (Toyapakeh) or Sanur (Bali) in outboard boats or small motorboats. The fare should be negotiated in advance.

The main attractions for visitors are the beautiful **beaches** and the reefs, which offer excellent conditions for swimming and snorkelling. Windsurfers favour the bay at the village of Jungutbatu. The Sea Temple at Jungutbatu is of interest only to specialists.

Petulu

See Ubud, Surroundings

Pujung

See Tampaksiring, Surroundings

Pulukan

See Negara, Surroundings

Pura (= "temple")

Pura Beji: see Singaraja, Surroundings
Pura Besakih: see Besakih
Pura Gunung Kawi Sebatu: see Tampaksiring, Surroundings
Pura Kehen: see Bangli
Pura Luhur Batukau: see Tabanan, Surroundings
Pura Luhur Ulu Watu: see Bukit Badung Peninsula
Pura Meduwe Karang: see Kubutambahan
Pura Tanah Lot: see Tabanan, Surroundings
Pura Tegeh Koripan: see Penelokan, Surroundings
Pura Tirtha Empul: see Tampaksiring, Surroundings
Pura Ulun Danu: see Bedugul, Surroundings

Puri (= "palace")

Puri Agung: see Klungkung, Kerta Gosa
Puri Agung Kanginan: see Amlapura
Puri Anyur / Puri Gede: see Tabanan, Surroundings, Krambitan
Puri Artha Sastra: see Bangli
Puri Gianyar: see Gianyar
Puri Pemecutan: see Denpasar

Sambiran

See Kubutambahan, Surroundings

Sangeh (Monkey Forest)

See Mengwi, Surroundings

Sangsit

See Singaraja, Surroundings

Sanur

See Denpasar, Surroundings

Sawan

See Singaraja, Surroundings

Singaraja   K 2

Region: North Bali
District: Budeleng
Altitude: 15 m (50 ft)
Population: 27,000

Access

By road: from Denpasar north via Sempidi, Mengwi and Bedugul; or – a
much more attractive route – Denpasar to Kapal, then west via Antosari
to Pengastulan and along the coast via Lovina Beach.
Bus: regular services daily from Denpasar-Ubung.
Bemo: on coast road to Lovina Beach.

Singaraja, chief town of Buleleng district and Bali's second largest town,
lies on the north coast of the island just under 80 km (50 mi.) from
Denpasar. In the fertile surrounding area there are extensive coffee plantations. The new harbour to the west of the town plays an important part
in Bali's trade with other Indonesian islands.

History The area around Singaraja seems to have been settled as early
as the 10th century, but it was only towards the end of the 16th century,
in the reign of Raja Panji Sakti, that the town became a place of any real
consequence. It was named Singaraja after the palace built by the Raja

Gitgit Waterfall
Bedugul, Denpasar

in 1604. The Buleleng district takes its name from a type of grain which was grown here in the late medieval period.

During the Dutch efforts to gain control of Bali Singaraja played a part of some importance, and it was only in 1849, after several unsuccessful attempts, that the Dutch managed to capture the stronghold. Later the town became the headquarters of the Dutch colonial administration, and remained the island's capital until 1946, when it gave place to Denpasar (see entry).

Sights

The original town of Singaraja lies a little inland, with the districts of Pegulangan and Pabeanbuleleng to the north. It is a less bustling town than the present capital, Denpasar.

Features of interest in Pabeanbuleleng are a charming Chinese temple (usually closed) on the Old Harbour, two small mosques and the lively Great Market (Tama Lila) held daily in Jalan Ahmad Yani.

The Pura Dalem, one of the most interesting Hindu temples in northern Bali is in Jalan Gajah Mada.

★★Pura Dalem

A small split gate leads into the first courtyard, which contains few buildings of any great interest. To the left is another richly decorated gate giving access to the second courtyard, which, surprisingly, is some 2 m (6½ ft) lower. On the left-hand side of this is the Bale Gong, on the right-hand side the Bale Pemalaiyagan, in which the gods are received

Chinese temple, Singaraja-Pabeanbuleleng

when they attend festivals in the temple. On the right of the wall between the first and second courtyards is a raised seat for the priests, and adjoining this an offering stand. At the far end of the temple complex steps lead up to a stone terrace, on which are *gedongs* dedicated to various divinities. Throughout the inner temple precinct and on the outer walls are finely executed reliefs which merit close attention.

★★Gedong Kirtya Library

Open Mon.–Fri. 8am–3pm

Admission charge

A visit to the Gedong Kirtya Library in Jalan Veteran can be recommended to those are interested in Balinese history and have some knowledge of Dutch.

The library contains some 3000 old manuscripts written on leaves of the *lontar* palm and numerous diaries, newspapers and periodicals dating from the period of Dutch occupation. These modern publications are in poor condition and already show signs of disintegration. Only the palm-leaf manuscripts are kept in lead boxes; the other material – arranged in a rather haphazard way – is on open shelves.

But if you have time at your disposal or are prepared to spend a rainy day on an excursion into the history of Bali you may well make some interesting discoveries in the Gedong Kirtya Library. The staff allow visitors access to almost all the library's holdings; and before leaving you will be expected to make an entry in the visitors' book and offer an appropriate financial contribution.

Surroundings

Lovina Beach

10 km (6 mi.) west-south-west of Singaraja, on the shores of the Bali Sea, is the resort of Lovina Beach, with a number of new hotels. Although the quality of the beach is not particularly high – it is narrow,

Komala Tirtha: hot springs and ...   *... bathing pool*

with dark-coloured sand – it is a pleasant enough place for a bathing holiday, much quieter than the crowded beaches of southern Bali.

Just to the west of Singaraja a side road branches off the road from Lovina Beach on the right (signposted "Air Panas") and comes in a few kilometres to Komala Tirtha, with hot sulphurous springs, beautifully situated in the forest. Visitors can bathe in the pools fed by the springs.

Komala Tirtha

Admission charge

The Gitgit waterfall is near the village of Gitgit (10 km (6 mi.) south-east of Singaraja on the road to Bedugul), in dense jungle.

★**Gitgit**

At the village of Sangsit, 6 km (4 mi.) north-east of Singaraja, is the lavishly decorated Pura Beji, a temple dedicated to the fertility and rice goddess Dewi Sri which belongs to a rice-farmers' co-operative (*subak*). The temple shows Chinese as well as Hindu features. The tripartite split gate leading into the inner courtyard is exceptionally richly ornamented; on its outer surface are several grimacing demons framed in finely carved lotus blossoms. Beyond the gate is an *aling-aling* (protective wall to keep out demons) flanked by two snakes. The profusion of carved ornament characteristic of northern Bali continues in the inner courtyard. Above the temple rears the *gedong* of the goddess Dewi Sri.

★**Sangsit**

On leaving the temple note the three figures from the "Ramayana" on each side.

Sangsit's other temple, the **Pura Dalem**, is relatively plain but is notable for its finely carved reliefs.

10 km (6 mi.) south of Sangsit is the village of Sawan, which is famed for the manufacture of gongs.

Sawan

Sukawati

Region: Central Bali
District: Gianyar
Altitude: 95 m (310 ft). Population: 12,000

Access

By road: from Denpasar north-east on the Gianyar road.
Bus: regular services daily from Denpasar–Kereneng.
Bemo: on the roads from Denpasar and Gianyar.

The town of Sukawati lies 17 km (11 mi.) north-east of Denpasar. Actually it is a double town, for Sukawati has been for centuries so closely joined to its neighbour to the north, Batuan, that the boundary between the two can be recognised only by natives of the town. A decree issued by Prince Marakata in 1022 ordered that the two towns should be separated, but the decree was never put into effect. The present-day population includes many Chinese, who have left their stamp on the town.

Neither in Sukawati nor in Batuan are there any tourist sights in the ordinary sense.

Crafts

Sukawati and Batuan are famed for the numerous craftsmen who offer their products for sale in the main streets of the double town. The crafts practised here have a long tradition behind them – in earlier times many famous artists worked in the palace of the Raja of Sukawati.

Balinese markets offer a rich array of textiles

In the centre of Sukawati is the Art Market, where a wide range of craft products can be bought.

Batuan is widely known for the characteristic style of painting developed here. Works in this style, which came increasingly to the fore around 1920, are less concerned with mythological and religious themes than with expressionistic representations of scenes from the life of the Balinese population. The artists working in this style, who had previously regarded the particular subject of a picture as merely accessory to the much more important background, now altered the balance of their work and increasingly concentrated their attention on the figure or landscape forming the main theme of the picture.

This change in style, which took place during the period of Dutch rule, is attributed to the fact that work was commissioned from the local artists by the new colonial rulers, who introduced them to European painting techniques.

The Batuan style later gained in influence when artists as well as tourists came to Bali from the West and began to teach the local painters. Among them were two artists whose reputation still stands high, Walter Spies (see Famous People) and Rudolf Bonnet.

Around Sukawati and Batuan are a number of other villages (e.g. Puaya) with large numbers of craftsmen.

Tabanan   K 7

Region: South Bali
District: Tabanan
Altitude: 105 m (345 ft)
Population: 12,000

Terraced fields, Tabanan

Tabanan

Access

By road: from Denpasar take the Gilimanuk and Negara road.
Bus and bemo: good services daily from Denpasar-Ubung.

Tabanan, chief town of the district of the same name, lies 24 km (15 mi.) north-west of Denpasar in a fertile and intensively cultivated region, known as the "rice granary of Bali".

History The town, or rather its rulers, played an important part during the period when the Dutch were attempting to occupy Bali. A powerful princedom from its earliest days, Tabanan retained its power for centuries and developed, particularly during the reign of Gusti Pandji Sakti (c. 1700), into one of the most influential princedoms on Bali.

When the Dutch landed on the north coast of Bali on June 22nd 1846 the Balinese forces could hold out only for a few days, and the princes of Bali went into hiding in the mountains. The declaration of one Raja is still remembered: "So long as I live this state will never recognise the sovereignty of Holland. Better that the kris should decide." When Dutch forces finally captured Tabanan and stood at the gates of the palace the members of the princely family did indeed take up their krises and commit ritual suicide (*puputan*).

Apart from a number of temples **the town** has no sights of particular interest: these are to be found in the surrounding area. The busy market (*pasar*) near the bemo station, however, is well worth a visit. Tabanan is also famed for its excellent gamelan orchestra. There is a Christian mission station in the town.

On the eastern outskirts of the town is a small but interesting Rice Museum which presents an excellent picture of rice cultivation on Bali.

Surroundings

★★**Scenery** The road north from Tabanan in the direction of Singaraja runs through an upland region of breathtaking beauty, passing intricately patterned rice terraces and busy little villages with friendly inhabitants. It is worth allowing plenty of time for the trip, with leisure to take in the varied impressions which this beautiful landscape affords.

★★**Krambitan**

A few kilometres south-west of Tabanan the large village of Krambitan has two interesting princely palaces, the Puri Anyar and the Puri Gede. Both palaces are directly on the village street.

Puri Anyar

The Puri Anyar is a faithful reconstruction of a palace originally built in the 17th century but largely destroyed in an earthquake. It is now a hotel, set in a beautiful tropical garden. Visitors may be allowed to look round the palace, which is laid out round a number of courtyards, even if they are not staying in it.

Puri Gede

Opposite the Puri Anyar is the Puri Gede, built in the second third of the 18th century in typical Balinese style. It can be seen by appointment.

★★**Pura Luhur Batukau**

28 km (17 mi.) north of Tabanan on a good road, at the foot of Gunung Batukau (2276 m (7468 ft)), Bali's second highest mountain, stands the Pura Luhur Batukau, one of the six royal temples of Bali.

The extensive temple complex lies in a romantic jungle landscape, with the central shrine oriented on Gunung Batukau.

In front of the entrance to the first courtyard, to the left, is the little Pura Dalem. Its most notable feature being the stone throne of Batari Uma (here in his manifestation as Durga), with a figure of Vishnu mounted on the divine bird Garuda.

In the first of the temple's two courtyards, to right and left, are a number of *bales* in which offerings of flowers and fruit are prepared. The

Krambitan: garden gate and ...   *... interior of Puri Gede*

Entrance to the Pura Luhur Batukau

Bathing pool, Yeh Panas

second courtyard is entered through the traditional split gate (*candi bentar*), with intricately carved reliefs. In this courtyard are several *merus* dedicated to different divinities, with varying numbers of pagoda roofs (*tumpangs*). The tallest, in the centre, has seven tiers and is dedicated to Batara Panji Sakti. To the left of this is a three-tiered *meru* dedicated to the five gods of the directions (Shiva, Vishnu, Ishvara, Brahma and Mahadevi).

Annually in March thousands of pilgrims from all over Bali make their way to the Pura Luhur Batukau and for several days make offerings to the gods. At these times the temple, which is normally quiet and unfrequented, is a place of busy and colourful activity.

★**Yeh Panas**

Admission charge

7 km (4½ mi.) south of the village of Wangayagede are the hot sulphurous springs of Yeh Panas. The extensive bathing establishment which has recently been laid out here includes a large swimming pool, individual rooms with mineral baths, and a restaurant.

★★**Pura Tanah Lot**

If there is one sight on Bali which no visitor to the island should miss it is the Pura Tanah Lot. Every evening coach-loads of tourists from Kuta, Legian and Sanur make their way through a labyrinth of lanes lined by souvenir-sellers to enjoy the magnificent spectacle of the sun setting behind the little temple on a rocky islet off the coast.

The Pura Tanah Lot, which can be reached on foot at low tide, was built at the beginning of the 16th century by Pedanda Sakti Bau Rauh, a priest who was forced to flee from religious persecution on Java and founded several temples on Bali. There is a shrine dedicated to him in the Pura Tanah Lot. The tallest building within the temple precinct (which normally cannot be entered by non-Hindus) is a five-tiered meru, the abode of the divine trinity of Brahma, Vishnu and Shiva. Another shrine is believed to be inhabited by a sacred snake.

One of Bali's most important temples, the Pura Tanah Lot

The best view of the temple and of the sunset, for those who cannot get a place at the temple itself or on the invariably crowded viewing terrace, is to be had from a point rather farther away on the cliff-fringed coast.

Tamblingan, Lake

See Bedugul, Surroundings

Tampaksiring   M 6

Region: Central Bali
District: Gianyar
Altitude: 630 m (2065 ft)

By road: from Denpasar north via Celuk.   Access
Bus: direct services from Denpasar several times daily.
Bemo: not recommended (and not always available) from Denpasar; better services from Ubud.

The attraction which draws tourists to the modest little market village of Tampaksiring in central Bali, 78 km (48 mi.) north-east of Denpasar, is the Pura Tirtha Empul, one of the most important source sanctuaries on the island; but it is also noted for the fine wood and bone carvings produced by the villagers, which can be bought all over Bali but are to be found at the best, and probably also their cheapest, in the village itself.

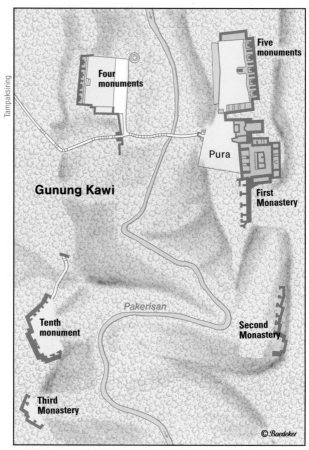

Sights

Tampaksiring is a typical central Balinese village with no particularly striking features.

★Pura Desa

The Pura Desa, a temple dedicated to Vishnu situated on the main road north, is worth a visit. In the first of its two courtyards are a number of pavilions with fine woodcarving and reliefs.

Surroundings

★Pujung

Like Tampaksiring, the village of Pujung is famed for the high quality of its woodcarving. The surrounding country is of great beauty, particularly when seen in the early morning.

★★Gunung Kawi

A few kilometres south of Tampaksiring on the Gianyar road is a religious site of an unusual type. In the narrow valley of the little river Pakerisan, below Gunung Kawi ("Mountain of Poetry"), are three groups of hermits' cells hewn from the rock, and three other groups of monuments whose date and function were for many years a mystery.

Various inscriptions, however, indicate that Anak Wungsu, at one time ruler of much of Bali, was venerated here together with his four wives and four concubines (who according to the legend committed suttee after his death). On this basis it appears that the complex was established in the 11th century, either in Anak's lifetime or soon after his death.

It was formerly believed, on the evidence of ashes found on the site, that the candis decorated with reliefs were the tombs of princes and princesses of divine status. Intensive research has shown this theory to be untenable, for closer examination of the ashes indicated that in all probability they came from the bones of animals sacrificed here to the spirits of the underworld.

Following the narrow path which runs down to the site from Tampaksiring, visitors first encounter a group of four monuments (perhaps for Anak's four concubines?). On the other bank of the stream, which here flows through scenery of particular beauty, is a further complex of buildings. To the left is a group of five monuments, one of which, higher than the others, may possibly be that of Anak Wungsu. To the right is a group of monks' cells known as the First Monastery, in the centre of which is a monolith of unknown significance. Farther down the gorge of the Pakerisan is a tenth monument (perhaps for a high official of Anak's court?). Above the east bank of the river and to the south of the tenth monument are two other groups of cells hewn from the rock, the Second and Third Monasteries.

The source sanctuary of Pura Gunung Kawi Sebatu is best reached by turning right off the road soon after leaving Tampaksiring and following

★ **Pura Gunung Kawi Sebatu**

The source sanctuary of Pura Gunung Kawi Sebatu

In the Pura Tirtha Empul

the signposts for 2.5 km (1½ mi.). Beyond a group of three ponds is the sanctuary itself, in the form of a square pool in the centre of which is a small open shrine containing a stone throne. Note particularly the pipes from which the water flows: although overgrown with moss in the course of years, they are still fine examples of Balinese stone-carving skill.

To one side is the main source sanctuary, Pura Sakti Puseh, which is always closed.

★★Pura Tirtha Empul

The origins of the source sanctuary of Pura Tirtha Empul are the subject of a legend. It is said that a demon named Vitra had gained possession of the water of all lakes and rivers and kept them locked up, so that there was a great drought. Then Indra drove a lance into the ground on the spot now occupied by the Tirtha Empul and opened up the springs, since when he has been known as the "guardian of the waters".

The central feature of the sanctuary is a lake which supplies water to four bathing pools. The water is discharged into the pools by 31 elaborately carved pipes.

The left-hand pool is for men, the right-hand one for women, for the performance of ritual purification. Once a year the people of the surrounding villages symbolically wash their pots, dishes and jars in the water.

In the small basin on the extreme right the "five sacred waters" (Pari Suda, Panglukatan, Sudamala, Tirtha Teteg and Bayan Cokor) are collected. In the centre of the basin is a *gedong* reserved for the god of the source sanctuary.

Many visitors take away supplies of water from the springs. The water is used for various purposes, including rites of passage.

Wisma Negara

On the hills above the temple is the Wisma Negara, a palace in modern style built by President Sukarno (see Famous People) in the 1950s as a summer residence. The palace is in two parts, separated from one another by a narrow valley but linked by a footbridge. It is now used as a government guest-house.

Visitors are admitted to the palace at certain times. An identification document must be produced, and there is a small admission charge.

From the spacious grounds of the palace there is a good view of the source sanctuary in the valley below.

Tanah Lot

See Tabanan, Surroundings

Tenganan   P 6

Region: East Bali
District: Karangasem
Altitude: 242 m (794 ft)
Population: about 450

By road: north-west from Candi Dasa.   Access
Bus and bemo: no regular services.
Ojek (motorcycle taxis): usually waiting on the roadside; fares are modest.

Tenganan lies under the south side of the central volcanic massif, the highest point in which is Gunung Agung. It is 4 km (2½ mi.) from Candi Dasa and 9 km (5½ mi.) from Amlapura.

The people of Tenganan occupy a special place in the **population** of Bali. They claim to have been created by the god Indra himself, and for proof of this refer to the "Usana Bali", a Balinese creation story written on palm-leaves in the 14th century, which states that the inhabitants of the village of Tenganan are descended from gods. The Bali Aga (Old Balinese) of Tenganan, like those of Trunyan (see Penelokan, Surroundings), form an independent community consisting of a number of groups organised in accordance with strict rules. They recognise no right of private property: everything belongs to the community. At the age of eight boys and girls must, after a transitional period of a year, join a group (*truna* or *daha*), and thereafter their family home is of only subordinate importance: the group is now responsible for bringing the children up to be full members of the community (*krama desa*). Later they are assigned, according to age, sex, occupation and capacity, to the "right" group, in which they remain for the rest of their lives.

As "favourites of the gods", the people of Tenganan see their aim in life not as strenuous physical labour but as the enjoyment of leisure, and also as the maintenance of old traditions and crafts. They let other people work for them: the rice-fields around the village are tended by peasants from other areas, who pay rent in the form of a proportion of the produce. The villagers of Tenganan thus have time to devote themselves to playing in gamelan orchestras, weaving fine textiles (this is the only place where the technique of double ikat is practised: see Art and Culture, Textiles) or copying old manuscripts. Any villagers who dissociate themselves from the community (for example by marrying someone from another village) lose all their rights as natives of the village. They may be allowed to remain in Tenganan but will be required to move to a section of the village to the east, Banjar Pande, and will not be permitted to take part in any religious ceremonies.

Children of Bali: a Hindu boy and ...   *... a girl dancing*

Sights

As recently as the early eighties visitors were unwelcome in Tenganan, but the villagers have now realised that tourism brings in good money and can improve still further their standard of living. Visitors are, however, still banned from entering any of the local temples.

Tenganan is a traffic-free area. Outside the village, which is surrounded by a wall, the local boys and girls lie in wait to act as guides.

The ★★**village** consists of three parallel streets aligned on Gunung Agung at one end and the sea at the other, along which are the family compounds, the houses and other buildings roofed with rice straw. Visitors will sometimes be invited into the compounds by the inhabitants. At the west end of the village stand the buildings in which the boys' and girls' groups meet and the Bale Agung, in which the (married) full members of the community meet.

Above the village are the Pura Sembangan (dedicated to Prince Pangus, an Old Balinese ruler) and the Pura Santi (the abode of the divinities of Gunung Agung).

Terima   C 2

Region: West Bali
District: Buleleng
Altitude: sea level

Access   By road: from Denpasar west along the coast.
                        Bus and bemo: good services from Gilimanuk and from Singaraja.

★★Bali Barat National Park

The Bali Barat (West Bali) National Park, established in 1983, has an area of 76,000 hectares (188,000 acres), taking in almost the whole of western Bali. Previously there had been a considerably smaller nature park established by the Dutch authorities.

Access The National Park can be reached from the village of Terima or from Gilimanuk or Singaraja. The headquarters of the National Park administration are in Cecek (4 km (2½ mi.) south of Gilimanuk), where visitors must pay the small admission charge for entry to the park.

Accommodation There are "homestays" and "losmens" (see Practical Information, Young People's Accommodation) in Gilimanuk, and there are also modest lodgings near the National Park offices.

Fauna Until about half a century ago the last tigers on Bali lived in the area now occupied by the National Park, and the park is still a refuge for species such as the banteng cattle of Bali, red deer and monkeys. Among the many species of birds is the now very rare and strictly protected Bali starling, which nests mainly in the northern part of the National Park. There are said to be only about 200 left, but since in spite of all appeals it is still being caught and offered for sale in local markets it is in danger of extinction within the foreseeable future. Bird-watchers will be delighted, however, by the great numbers of other tropical birds.

Lovers of unspoiled nature will enjoy **walking** in this great natural wilderness, though there are few paths and tracks, and those almost all in the north-western part of the National Park.

Landscape in western Bali

Menjangan

Off the coast at the north-western corner of the Bali Barat National Park is the uninhabited island of Menjangan. The boat trip from Terima takes about half an hour. Scuba divers and snorkellers will find a fascinating underwater world to explore off the shores of the island.

Trunyan

See Penelokan, Surroundings

Ubud   M 7

Region: Central Bali
District: Gianyar
Altitude: 92 m (302 ft)
Population: 16,000

Access

By road: from Denpasar north-east via Kesiman and Sukawati.
Bus: several services daily from Denpasar-Kereneng.
Bemo: not recommended from Denpasar.

Ubud, Bali's "artistic heart", lies 25 km (15 mi.) north-north-east of Denpasar on the southern edge of the central Balinese heartland, in a region of charming tropical landscape.
    The well watered soil, irrigated by an intricate network of canals, enabled the population for many centuries to prosper on the proceeds of agriculture; nowadays an increasing proportion of their income comes from the tourist trade.

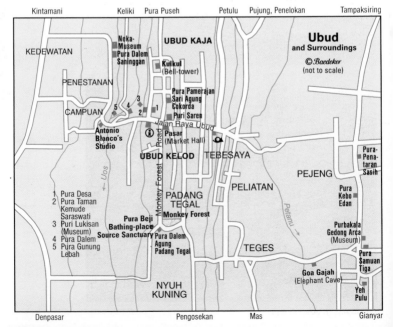

Arts and crafts Ubud is regarded as the artistic and cultural centre of Bali. Many artists still live here, finding their inspiration in the beautiful country around the town. Some of them – painters, sculptors, wood-carvers, etc. – have formed artistic communities.

Ubud and the surrounding area are a good "shopping centre" for traditional Balinese handicrafts; and with luck you may come upon some genuine antique – remembering that you require an export permit to take it home.

Although Ubud has little in the way of tourist sights to back up its attraction as an artistic centre, it is well provided with accommodation for visitors and makes a good base from which to explore the surrounding country.

Sights

Ubud has a number of charming **temples**, and there are a variety of temple festivals and other ceremonies throughout the year.

A visit to the Neka Museum, named after the Balinese painter Suteja Neka (b. 1939), can be recommended particularly to those interested in the development of painting on Bali. Neka inherited his talent in part from his father, a gifted sculptor and an active member of Bali's first artistic society who gained a certain reputation only in his later years. Suteja Neka's breakthrough came in 1966, when there was an exhibition of his and his father's works at the opening of a new hotel. Thereafter he devoted himself to teaching young Balinese the rudiments of painting. He was also an active collector of works of art created on Bali, including pictures by Walter Spies (see Famous People), Rudolf Bonnet and Miguel Covarrubias and many works by Balinese artists.

The Neka Museum has a total exhibition area of 6900 sq. m (74,300 sq.

★★Neka Museum

Open daily
8am–4pm

Admission charge

Washday, Ubud

ft) in four buildings set in a beautiful garden. A fifth building is used for temporary exhibitions.

A profusely illustrated guide to the museum, which gives biographies of the artists as well as information about the works on show, can be bought at the ticket office.

★Antonio María Blanco

Open daily 9am–5pm

Admission charge

A short distance west of the town centre, in a splendid tropical garden, is the house and studio of one of the best known painters on Bali, Antonio María Blanco (see Famous People). The pictures displayed in the house – many of them for sale – give an excellent overview of Blanco's varied artistic activity. The house, which was presented to the artist by the son of a Balinese prince, is now the headquarters of the Blanco Art Foundation.

★Monkey Forest

10 minutes' walk south of the town centre is the Monkey Forest, which is considerably smaller than the one at Sangeh (see Mengwi, Surroundings) but has a more beautiful setting.

After running the gauntlet of the inevitable peanut and souvenir sellers, visitors come to a gigantic *waringin* tree, under which is a stone figure of a monkey.

A temple on the west side of the Monkey Forest, the Pura Dalem Agung Padang Tegal, is the haunt of hundreds of little monkeys, which as a rule are happy to take food from visitors but can on occasion become unpleasantly aggressive. The temple itself is a good example of southern Balinese religious architecture: note particularly the covered gate (*candi korung*) and the bell-tower (*kulkul*), set on a stepped base and richly decorated with reliefs, with a striker in the form of a phallus.

Surroundings

Petulu

Bird-watchers will find it well worth while to make a detour to Petulu, only 3 km (2 mi.) north of Ubud. In the evening great flocks of white herons – a bird which to the Balinese is sacred – swoop down and settle on the trees around the village.

Mas

4 km (2½ mi.) south of Ubud is the little village of Mas, which is famed for the skill of its craftsmen. The main street of the village is lined with the shops and showrooms of woodcarvers, sculptors and other artists. Their workshops are often close by, enabling visitors to watch the craftsmen at work. Some woodcarvers runs courses for beginners and at a more advanced level.

Near the end of the village are the furniture-makers, who make tables, chairs and other items of bamboo and rattan.

West Bali National Park

See Terima

Evening on Lombok, looking across to Gunung Agung on Bali ▶

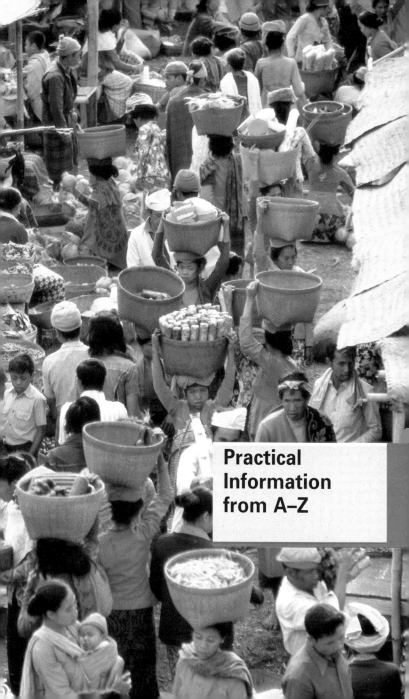

**Practical
Information
from A–Z**

Practical Information from A–Z

Air Travel

Garuda Indonesia, the Indonesian national airline, maintains a dense network of services, with which Denpasar airport on Bali is linked. In addition to numerous intercontinental connections with European and North American airports it flies regular services to other Indonesian airports such as Jakarta, Palembang, Surabaya and Yogyakarta, to the neighbouring countries of Malaysia and Singapore and to Bangkok, Manila, Hong Kong and Tokyo.

British Airways have daily flights to Jakarta (Java) via Singapore.

The Dutch airline KLM has traditionally played a major part in providing air services between Europe and Indonesia.

Air services within the Indonesian archipelago are flown by Garuda Indonesia and by three smaller airlines, Merpati, Sempati and Bouraq.

Air fares in Asia are generally lower than in Europe. Flights before and after public holidays and festivals are usually fully booked – indeed sometimes overbooked. Since flying is often the only means of travelling long distances quickly, air services perform a function in Indonesian social life (e.g. in facilitating visits to relatives).

Airports

Bali

Denpasar's Ngurah Rai Airport, named after an Indonesian freedom fighter, is situated 12 km (7½ mi.) south of Denpasar and 3 km (2 mi.) south of Kuta.

The left-hand part of the air terminal building is the Domestic Airport for flights within Indonesia; the right-hand part is the International Airport. The central section is the arrivals area.

In the arrivals hall are a hotel reservation desk (which will also arrange transport to the hotel), telephones and several exchange offices. (Before changing any large sums of money, check the exchange rates offered.)

Transfers

Transfers from and to the airport are usually arranged by the hotel or tour operator. Otherwise there is the Koperasi Taxi Service, which has a desk in the airport building – a co-operative of taxi-drivers which conveys passengers from the airport to destinations on Bali at fixed rates. The tariff is displayed at the desk, where the fare is paid; the driver receives only the receipt.

The journey is cheaper by bemo (see Public Transport). A bemo can be picked up a few hundred yards from the airport on the Denpasar road.

Lombok

Mataram Airport, on Lombok, is only a few kilometres north of the town of Mataram on the road to the resort of Senggigi Beach. It can be reached from the town only on taxis authorised to carry passengers to the airport. Visitors arriving at the airport, however, will find plenty of taxis waiting to take them to their hotel. Those travelling on a package holiday will be met by a representative of their tour operator outside the arrivals hall. For those arriving without a hotel reservation there is a hotel reservation desk in the arrivals hall.

◄ *Everywhere on Bali are colourful markets where local people and tourists can find everything to their heart's desire.*

An MD 11 of Garuda Indonesia

Porters are available at both airports. The charge is 1000 rupiahs per item of baggage.

Porters

During the main holiday periods (June/July, Christmas and before and after the Muslim fast month of Ramadan) flights on all Asian airlines tend to be fully booked, and often overbooked. Even if your air ticket is marked "OK", therefore, you should confirm your return flight with the airline (addresses below) at least two days in advance.

Return flights

For international flights passengers should check in two hours before departure time; for flights within Indonesia one hour is normally sufficient.

Check-in times

Prior to flying overseas airport charges must be paid in cash. At present these are some 20,000 rupiahs.

Airport charges

Airlines

Garuda Indonesia
35 Duke Street
London W1M 5DF
Tel. (0171) 9357055

United Kindom

British Airways
P. T. Kandida Persada
World Trade Centre Building (10th floor)
Jalan Jenderal, Sudirman Kav 29/31
Jakarta. Tel. (021) 5211492

On Bali (or in Jakarta)

155

Garuda Indonesia
Jalan Melati 01, Denpasar
Tel. 225245; return flight confirmations 234606
Office in Kuta Beach Hotel: tel. 751179

Merpati
Jalan Melati 57, Denpasar
Tel. 228842 and 222159

Bouraq
Jalan Kamboja, Denpasar
Tel. 223564

Sempati
Jalan Merdeka Timur 7, Jakarta
Tel. (021) 348760/367

Antiques

Genuine antiques are now rare on Bali, and it is only occasionally that visitors are likely to come across anything really old that is worth the money asked for it. The Balinese, however, are highly skilled in the manufacture of reproductions which are often difficult to distinguish from the real thing.

The export of antiques – defined in Indonesia as art objects more than 50 years old – is permitted only with a special authorisation. For information on the regulations, apply to the Government Tourist Office in Denpasar (see Information).

Bathing

Bali is not exactly a bathers' paradise. It has no beaches of white coral sand: the sand on Bali is mixed with volcanic ash or sometimes consists entirely of ash, giving it its dark colour. Those who do not mind this will find themselves well catered for at Kuta, Legian or Nusa Dua in southern Bali, Candi Dasa in eastern Bali and Lovina Beach in northern Bali. A sun cream with a high protection factor should be applied when swimming or snorkelling.

Warning

Beaches which are suitable for bathing and swimming are specially marked. Elsewhere bathing may be hazardous on account of heavy surf, which may be several metres high, and dangerous currents, not always detectable at first glance, which may bring even good swimmers into difficulties.

Bathers should therefore pay heed to the advice of local people and the warning signs on beaches not suitable for bathing.

The beaches are often polluted, and bathing shoes are a necessary precaution against broken glass and other litter as well as fragments of coral washed on to the shore.

Batik Courses

A piece of batik work you have done yourself makes an attractive souvenir of a visit to Bali. There are now organised courses, lasting a single

An alternative, relatively safe bathing-place

day or several days, which teach both traditional and modern batik techniques. For information, apply to your hotel reception or, for example to:
Apsari Batik Course
Buala Village, Nusa Dua. Tel. 71310
   A large number of Batik studios can also be found outside the centres of tourism, e.g. in Ubud. Here it is possible at any time to combine a visit to Bali with artistic activity under the guidance of an expert.

Begging

Visitors to Bali will encounter begging by children, and sometimes also by ill or disabled adults, especially in areas frequented by tourists. Particularly in the case of children – who are increasingly being exploited by adults who induce them to beg or to offer things for sale at inflated prices – it is important not to give money, since this merely encourages the abuse. Children will, however, appreciate some small gift such as a cake of soap or a ball-point pen.

Bemos

See Public Transport

Bicycle Rental

See Car Rental

Boat Charter

Around Bali there are excellent sailing waters, but there are few firms from whom boats can be chartered. Usually a local crew must be hired with the boat.

One- and two-day cruises on "Ocean Lady II" from Nusa Dua in Sanur Bay and to the island of Lembongan are run by:

P. T. Tourdevco Operation
Denpasar. Tel. 287739 and 231591

Breakdown Assistance

See Motoring

Buses

See Public Transport

Business Hours

In Indonesia, as in many other Asian countries, there are no statutory shop closing times. There are thus no restrictions on the energy and enterprise of individual traders. Many shops, particularly in areas frequented by visitors, are open until late in the evening, giving their customers plenty of time for shopping. On Sundays and public holidays, however, many shops are closed.

Business hours — Banking hours are Mon.–Fri. 8am–12am, Sat. 8am–11am. Exchange bureaux are usually open daily from 8am–8pm.

Chemists — Daily 9am–7pm, sometimes to 8pm.

Exchange offices — Usually open daily 8am–8pm.

Post offices — See Postal Services and Telecommunications

Shops — 9am–8pm; in tourist areas until late in the evening.

Calendars

In addition to the Gregorian calendar there are three other calendar systems in use on Bali. The Uku and Saka systems play an important part in determining the dates of religious festivals, but their structure and operation are so complicated that only Brahmans and special astrologers are able to interpret these calendars, so very different from western systems. The other system is the Islamic calendar, which is of less importance on this mainly Hindu island.

Uku calendar — The Uku (Javanese-Balinese) calendar is based on a year of 210 days, consisting of 30 seven-day weeks. This calendar is used for determining the date of almost all events of importance in the Balinese year, in particular the various "birthdays" which are celebrated in the course of a year. Not only people have birthdays: different professional groups – rice-farmers and artists, craftsmen and intellectuals – all have their birthdays, and so do agricultural implements, weapons, motor-cars and machines.

A propitious date must be determined for those events which are of prime importance to a population still predominantly engaged in farming, such as the days on which the rice harvest may begin and must end. And of course the best times must be fixed for the numerous temple festivals, the most important of which are the festivals of the royal temples.

The fixing of these birthdays calls for long and complicated calculations and observations to determine a propitious day, which in the following year may be quite different.

As a result of the different length of year the Javanese-Balinese calendar is at present 78 years behind the Gregorian calendar used in the West.

The Saka (Hindu-Balinese) calendar is more similar to the Gregorian, but is based on the phases of the moon. The year (*caka*) consists of twelve months of 29 or 30 days; and since this year is out of line with the astronomical year an additional intercalary month is inserted every 30 months.

Saka calendar

The Hindu faith, properly speaking, recognises no count of years, since for the Hindu all that happens is a continuous process, caught up in an eternally recurring cycle: there is thus no year 0.

The Muslim calendar is of relatively limited importance on Bali, though it plays a larger role on Lombok. It is based on the Arab calendar, which is a lunar one. The year has 354 days, divided into twelve months of 29 or 30 days. The divergence from the astronomical year is corrected by the insertion of intercalary years.

Muslim calendar

Sarongs must be worn at a temple festival

Muslim chronology begins with the year of Mohammed's flight from Mecca to Medina, the Hejira (A.D. 622 = year 1).

In the public life of Indonesia, including Bali and Lombok, the western calendar is completely accepted.

Western calendar

Camping

There are no official camping sites on Bali or Lombok. Backpackers are not now welcomed on Bali, and although "wild" camping in open country is not officially prohibited it is frowned on. There is, however, plenty of cheap accommodation available outside the tourist areas, for example in "homestays", "losmens" and "penginapans" (see Young People's Accommodation).

Car Rental

One way of exploring Bali or Lombok is in a rented car. On both islands, but particularly on Bali, there are numerous car rental firms, mostly offering four-wheel-drive vehicles (jeeps) of Japanese origin (mainly Suzukis).

Cars

Drivers must be at least 21 years of age, and will usually be asked to produce an international driving licence. They must be prepared to cope with unfamiliar driving conditions and with the sometimes anarchic driving methods of the locals.

Extreme caution is necessary in driving on Bali and Lombok, and driving at night should be avoided if at all possible. It is a good idea to hire a local driver with the car; it will not cost much, and he will have the advantage of knowing the country and the mentality of the Balinese. Although Indonesian legislation makes drivers fully responsible for their behaviour on the road, some drivers like to demonstrate their skill to their passengers. In these circumstances the phrase "Pelan-pelan!" ("Slow! slow!") may be found useful.

On taking over a rented car you should make sure that it is fit to drive (condition of brakes, tyres, lighting, etc.) and should check for any damage it has previously suffered. You should also confirm that the vehicle has full insurance cover. The safest way is to go to a reputable rental firm.

The hire of a motorcycle is to be recommended only for experienced riders, and even they will find motorcycling on Bali or Lombok hazardous, as a result of the lamentable condition of many roads, particularly in the interior (potholes, sudden changes of surface, treacherous road-holding after rain), and of local motorcycling techniques, which lead every year to numerous accidents.

Motorcycles

It should be mentioned for the sake of completeness that a driving licence for a motorcycle can be obtained very quickly and easily on Bali. It is necessary only to go to the police station in Denpasar (in Jalan Raya Kuta), pay a modest fee, demonstrate a knowledge of road signs and pass a practical test, which involves performing a figure of eight without allowing the feet to touch the ground.

A bicycle is an ideal way of getting to know Bali, and there are now increasing numbers of firms offering bicycles to rent, particularly in the tourist centres of Sanur, Kuta and Legian and in Denpasar. Some hotels also have bicycles to rent (often including mountain bikes).

Pedal cycles

◀ *The dates of temple festivals are calculated according to the Balinese calendar*

Before renting a bicycle you should of course check it for safety (brakes, lights).

Organised cycle tours with mountain bikes (e.g. on the "Batur Trail") are run by:
Sobek Expeditions
Jalan Bypass Ngurah Rai 56 X
Sanur. Tel. 287059

Chemists

There are numerous chemists' shops on Bali, particularly in tourist areas; they can be recognised by the sign "Apotik" or "Toko Obat". They stock a selection of medicines in current use, some of them under names used only in Asia.

If you are dependent on particular medicines you should take a sufficient supply with you on holiday, or if buying them locally should check by comparison with the original pack that the product sold in Indonesia is identical with the one you require. If in doubt consult a doctor (see Illness).

Medicines in Indonesia, as elsewhere in Asia, are considerably cheaper than in the West.

Opening times   See Business Hours

Churches

See Religious Services

Consulates

See Embassies and Consulates

Credit Cards

See Currency

Currency

Currency   The Indonesian unit of currency is the rupiah (Rp).

Coins   There are coins in denominations of 5, 10, 25, 50 and 100 rupiahs.

Banknotes   There are banknotes for 100, 500, 1000, 5000 and 10,000 rupiahs.

Exchange rate   The exchange rate for banks is officially laid down and is posted daily in banks and in leading newspapers. It is applied at the exchange desks of the Bank Negara Indonesia (BNI) in towns, at airports and in the interior of the island. Other exchange offices (money changers) are likely to give a rather better rate. This is already obvious on arrival at Ngurah Rai airport where the exchange bureaux in the airport sometimes offer a rate considerably inferior to that of those in the arrival hall. Money should not be changed at hotels, which usually offer a poorer rate, except in an emergency.

Indonesian money

Rupiahs will be changed back only if you can produce a receipt for the original exchange.

There are no restrictions on the import of foreign currency. Indonesian currency can be taken in or brought out up to a limit of 50,000 rupiahs per person; the limit can be exceeded only with a special authorisation.

It is advisable to bring some Indonesian currency from home for immediate expenses on arrival (taxi or bus fares, tips, etc.). You should make sure that the banknotes you bring with you from home, or acquire after arrival, are in good condition, since damaged or unduly dirty notes may not be accepted.

It is also a good idea to carry enough rupiahs in small denominations, since taxi drivers and small shops, for example, may not always have change and it would otherwise be necessary to round up a payment more than you would wish.

It is best to carry money in the form of travellers' cheques, both because of their greater security and because they attract a better exchange rate. In case of loss or theft they can be quickly replaced provided that proper care has been exercised (e.g. by keeping the cheques separate from the receipt for their purchase). Dollar cheques are most widely acceptable, though it is generally possible to cash sterling cheques in tourist areas.

Eurocheques cannot be used on Bali or Lombok.

The major credit cards – American Express, BankAmericard/Visa, Mastercard/Eurocard, Diners Club – are accepted, particularly in the tourist areas, by shops, duty-free shops at airports, banks, travel agencies, airlines and hotels. Car rental firms accept credit cards only if they belong to an international chain.

If you lose a credit card you must at once inform the issuing agency by telephone. You should take a note of its telephone number before leaving home and keep it separate from the card.

Failing this, local credit card agencies are: American Express, c/o Pacto Ltd., Bali Beach Hotel, Sanur, tel. 288449; Bank Americard Visa, c/o Bank Duta, Jalan Hayam Waruk, tel. 226578 and 231481; Diners Club, c/o Pt. Diners Jaya Indonesia (in Jakarta), tel. (021) 5701340; Mastercard/Eurocard, c/o Bank Central Asia Card Center (in Jakarta), tel. (021) 5701878.

Banks

On Bali and Lombok the Negara Indonesia (BNI), Niaga and Dagang Negara Banks, with branches in at least the larger towns, can carry out all normal financial transactions.

Opening times

See Business Hours

Telegraphic drafts

Money can be transferred by telegraph between western countries and Indonesia, but the process takes at least two days. When collecting the money the recipient will be required to produce his passport.

Customs Regulations

Entering Indonesia

The following goods may be imported duty-free: personal effects in appropriate quantity; cigarettes (maximum 200), 50 cigars, 100 grams of tobacco, 2 litres of wine or spirits, two cameras together with film, a film or video camera.

The import of narcotics, communist or pornographic literature, hunting guns and ammunition is strictly forbidden. Visitors to Bali generally pass quickly through customs.

Re-entry into EU countries

The import of plants, animals or products made from plants and animal parts which are protected under the CITES agreement (also known as the Washington Species Protection Agreement) is forbidden. As far as Bali and Indonesia are concerned this includes corals, (particularly the black coral), reptiles (especially geckos), turtles and tortoises (including turtle and tortoise shell), birds and products made from protected plants.

On re-entering EU countries directly from Indonesia or states not belonging to the European Union (EU) souvenirs and presents with a total value of £125 are duty-free. Persons over 15 years may import 500 grams of coffee or 200 grams of instant coffee, 50 grams of perfume and 0.25 litre toilet water and persons over 17 years 1 litre of spirits with an alcohol content above 22 per cent or 2 litres of sparkling wine or 2 litres of wine as well as 200 cigarettes or 100 cigarillos or 50 cigars or 250 grams of tobacco.

Dances

Performances of Balinese dances are now frequently put on for the benefit of tourists – though it is perhaps a question how far performances of this kind have anything to do with the traditions of Balinese dance. It is increasingly difficult for visitors to see dances uninfluenced by commercial considerations, since they are usually performed in the evening or sometimes at night, when the tourists are back in their hotels. Away from the tourist track you may be fortunate enough to come on a village

Scene from the Barong dance

where dances are still performed in the traditional way and, with friendly villagers, may be invited to attend a local festival.

At Bali's many festivals and other celebrations traditional dances including the *kecak*, the Barong dance, the kris dance and the frog dance are performed, as well as extracts from the "Ramayana" epic. The times of these events can be obtained from tour operators and hotel reception desks.

In the Werdi Budaya Art Centre in Denpasar there are public rehearsals every morning by young dancers in training, and daily at 6.30pm there is a performance of the Barong dance (admission charge).

Werdi Budaya Art Centre

Distances

The table on p. 166 shows the distances, in kilometres, between selected towns and villages on Bali.

Dress

Light-weight cotton clothing allowing the circulation of air is best in the tropical climate of Bali at any time of year; synthetic fibres should be avoided. For the "cooler" months and for excursions in the mountains something warmer (a sweater or woollen jacket) should be included in your luggage.

Distances, in kilometres, between selected places on Bali	Amlapura	Bangli	Bedugul	Candi Dasa	Celuk	Denpasar	Gianyar	Gilimanuk	Kintamani	Klungkung	Kuta	Mas	Mengwi	Negara	Penelokan	Sangeh	Sanur	Singaraja	Tabanan	Tampaksiring	Ubud
Amlapura	•	56	126	20	67	78	51	206	79	38	87	62	94	173	78	99	81	137	99	65	61
Bangli	55	•	88	35	29	40	13	168	28	18	49	27	56	135	20	61	43	80	61	32	23
Bedugul	126	88	•	106	59	48	75	148	116	88	57	70	32	115	112	50	55	30	43	85	73
Candi Dasa	20	35	106	•	70	58	31	186	66	18	67	45	74	153	58	79	61	124	79	51	41
Celuk	67	29	59	70	•	12	16	139	57	29	21	50	27	106	76	32	14	89	32	26	46
Denpasar	78	39	49	68	12	•	27	128	68	40	9	22	16	95	64	21	7	78	21	37	25
Gianyar	51	13	75	31	16	27	•	155	41	13	36	11	43	122	33	48	30	93	48	15	10
Gilimanuk	206	168	148	186	139	128	155	•	196	168	137	157	144	33	192	107	135	85	107	165	153
Kintamani	86	28	116	66	57	68	41	196	•	48	86	44	84	163	8	89	72	52	89	28	48
Klungkung	38	18	88	18	29	40	13	168	48	•	49	24	56	135	40	61	43	100	61	27	23
Kuta	87	49	57	77	21	9	36	137	70	49	•	31	25	104	73	30	8	87	30	46	34
Mas	62	27	70	45	50	22	11	157	44	24	31	•	38	117	76	50	25	104	43	19	4
Mengwi	94	56	32	74	27	16	43	144	84	56	25	38	•	83	81	37	23	62	9	53	41
Negara	173	135	115	153	106	95	122	33	163	135	104	117	83	•	159	116	102	112	74	132	120
Penelokan	78	20	112	58	76	64	33	192	8	40	73	76	81	159	•	81	71	60	85	23	40
Sangeh	99	61	50	79	32	21	48	107	89	61	30	50	37	116	81	•	28	99	42	61	46
Sanur	81	43	55	61	14	7	30	135	72	43	8	25	23	102	71	28	•	85	28	40	28
Singaraja	137	80	30	117	89	78	93	85	52	100	87	104	62	112	60	99	85	•	73	110	100
Tabanan	99	61	43	79	32	21	48	107	89	61	30	43	9	74	85	42	28	73	•	48	46
Tampaksiring	65	32	85	45	26	37	15	165	28	27	46	19	53	132	23	61	40	110	48	•	15
Ubud	61	23	73	41	46	25	10	153	48	23	34	4	41	120	40	46	28	100	46	15	•

Official occasions

In general the Balinese prefer casual dress, though a jacket and tie are worn in important business dealings. But for a visit to a government office a T-shirt and shorts are frowned on, for the Balinese attach importance to etiquette on official occasions. It is important, above all, to avoid any possibility of being taken for one of the backpacking tourists who are not welcomed in Indonesia.

Visiting temples

T-shirt and shorts should not be worn when visiting a temple, since this would offend the religious sensibilities of the Balinese. Women should cover their shoulders and men wear long trousers. Before entering the precincts of a temple visitors must wrap a selendang, a kind of shawl or scarf, round their waist. At a temple festival the wearing of a sarong is obligatory for both men and women. The selendang and sarong can either be bought at the beginning of your visit to Bali or hired, for a small charge, at the temple.

Drugs

In Indonesia, as in almost all Asian countries, the use of drugs and, still more, dealing in drugs are subject to heavy penalties. The import and export of narcotics is strictly prohibited, and even their possession is an offence.

Foreigners offending against the drug laws are normally sentenced to long periods of imprisonment, and in extreme cases the death penalty may be imposed.

On no account should you agree to carry anything out of the country on behalf of anyone else. In the past misplaced kindness in this respect has brought innocent travellers under suspicion as drug couriers.

Electricity

Electricity on Bali is normally 220 volts 50 cycles, though in some outlying districts it may be 110 volts. For most western visitors an adaptor is needed.

Embassies and Consulates

Indonesian Embassies

38 Grosvenor Square London W1X 9AD. Tel. (0171) 4997661	United Kingdom
2020 Massachusetts Avenue NW Washington DC 20036. Tel. (202) 7755200	United States
55 Parkdale Avenue Ottawa, Ontario K1Y IE5. Tel. (613) 7241100	Canada
8 Darwin Avenue Yarralumla, Canberra ACT 2600, Tel. (06) 2508600	Australia
70 Glen Road Kelburn, Wellington. Tel. (47) 58697/98/99	New Zealand

Embassies in Indonesia

Jalan M. H. Thamrin 75 Jakarta. Tel. 330904	United Kingdom
Jalan Merdeka Selatan 5 Jakarta. Tel. 360360	United States
Metropolitan Building 1 (5th floor) Jalan Jendral Sudirman 29 Jakarta. Tel. 510709	Canada
Jalan M. H. Thamrin 15 Jakarta. Tel. 323109	Australia
Jalan Diponegoro 41 Jakarta. Tel. 330680	New Zealand

Consulates on Bali

Jalan Raya Sanur 146 Tanjung Bungkak, Denpasar Tel. 35092 and 35093	Australia

The Australian consulate also handles the affairs of citizens of the United Kingdom, Canada and New Zealand, which have no consulates on Bali.

United States

Jalan Segara Ayu-Sanur 5
Denpasar
Tel. 88478

Emergencies

Emergency
service on Bali

P. T. Bali Tourist International Assistance
Tel. 227271, 228996 and 231443

Police

On Bali, tel. 110; on Lombok, tel. 51998

Fire

On Bali, tel. 113 or 15113; on Lombok, tel. 113

Ambulance

On Bali, tel. 188 or 199

Events

The Bali Government Tourist Office in Denpasar and the Regional Tourism Office in Mataram on Lombok (see Information) publish calendars giving the times of religious and cultural events. This information can also be obtained by enquiry at hotel reception desks or from the "Bali Echo", an English-language tourist magazine.

Ferry Services

Ferry ports

Between Bali and Java and between Bali and Lombok there are regular services, several times daily, by car ferries and hydrofoils ("jetfoils"). The ferries to Java (Ketapang, the island's most easterly port) sail from Gilimanuk, at the western tip of Bali, those to Lombok (Lembar, south of Mataram) from Benoa (south of Denpasar). There are boats to Bali's offshore islands of Lembongan (Jungutbatu) and Penida (Toyapakeh) from Benoa, Sanur, Kusamba and Padang Bai.

Bookings can be made at travel agencies, the ports of departure or the shipping companies.

Bali–Java

See Getting to Bali

Bali–Lombok (at
least twice daily)

P. T. Mabua Intan Express
Benoa Harbour (Bali)
Tel. 72521

Lembar Harbour (Lombok)
Tel. (0364) 25895

Bali–Penida

See Sights from A to Z, Penida, Transport

Bali–Lembongan

See Sights from A to Z, Penida, Lembongan.

The 34 m (112 ft) luxury catamaran "Bali Hai" plies regularly between Benoa and Lembongan. Bookings for day trips and "dinner cruises" (2½ hours):
Bali Hai Cruises, Benoa Harbour
Tel. 234331

Ferry in Padang Bai harbour

Festivals and Public Holidays

Festivals on Bali

It is scarcely possible to spend any time on Bali without seeing a festival of some kind. Somewhere on the island there is bound to be a "birthday" celebration at some temple, and as you go about the island this will be obvious by the sight of the gaily decorated temples and the fairs held in front of them.

In the long series of festivals, mainly of a religious nature, celebrated throughout the year there is no conflict between different religions: even the festivals and holidays of another faith are an opportunity for lively celebrations as well as an occasion for meditation. And if you stay long enough on the island at the right time of year you will be able to celebrate the New Year three times – in the western, Chinese and Balinese fashions.

The traditional cremation of the dead is accompanied on Bali by elaborate rituals (see Facts and Figures, Religion, Cremation).   Cremation

The "birthday" of a temple, commemorating its original consecration, is celebrated in an elaborate festival (*odalan*) on a date fixed by a priest after complicated calculations based on the Balinese calendar (see Calendars). The festival always lasts three days (see Facts and Figures, Religion, Temple Festivals).   Temple birthdays

According to an unofficial estimate there are well over a thousand festivals on Bali in the course of the year. Only a few of the most important festivals are included in the following listing of public holidays.

Oggo-Oggo an Nyepi

Each country celebrates the New Year in its own way. In the West we like to take a cheerful farewell of the departing year and give a noisy welcome to the new one. It is very different on Bali. There can surely be no other place on earth where the transition from one year to another is celebrated in the same style as on the island of gods, spirits and demons.

The Balinese celebrate their New Year festival – **Nyepi** – at the spring equinox, but preparations for the celebration begin many weeks in advance. They involve fierce competition between the young people of Bali – at any rate between the boys. The object is to construct on a bamboo frame, using wood, papier-mâché, paste and paint, an outsize monster – **Oggo-Oggo** – which shall be more terrifying than the one made by the boys of the next village. Spirits are well known to be hardened to fear, and so any demon made by human hands must look even wilder and more fearsome than the most evil spirit. The contest, however, is a cheerful one, not taken too seriously by the boys – though their elders may perhaps sometimes seek to stimulate their ambition.

Three days before the New Year festival, on Saka Day, thousands of festively dressed Balinese make their way to the coasts of the island and deposit offerings on the shore designed to earn the favour of the spirits and demons during the coming year. The celebrations at Sanur are particularly spectacular. (Visitors must remember to wear a sarong.)

On Pengerupuk Day, the last day of the year, the Balinese bring purification offerings to ensure that their island shall be spotlessly clean. Some days earlier long bamboo poles decorated with yellow and white ribbons have been set up in the streets to assure the gods that they will be welcome at the festival.

On New Year's night there are great processions, to which the constructors of the monsters in particular look forward eagerly. The largest and most colourful processions are at Kuta and Denpasar, where the streets are lined with thousands of spectators. No less interesting, and perhaps rather more spontaneous, are the processions in the villages of the interior.

The Nyepi festival reaches its climax on New Year's night. When darkness falls the Oggo-Oggo figures – some of them rather rickety – are paraded about the streets by their constructors, preceded by musicians making a deafening noise. Any evil spirits which are not wakened up and frightened by the noise into taking their departure must be tough indeed ...

The Balinese, however, like to make sure. Since they cannot be absolutely certain that some particularly stubborn spirit has not withstood this exorcism, they make it appear on the following day that Bali is completely uninhabited. On that day no fires and no lights may be lit, no one may move about the streets and all work comes to a standstill. Even tourists may not leave their hotel.

A fearsome Oggo-Oggo and his proud constructors ▶

Fixed public holidays on Bali

January 1st	New Year's Day (western).
April 21st	Kartini Day (comparable with Mother's Day in the West).
August 17th	Indonesian National Day (Proklamasi Kemerdekaan = Declaration of Independence, 1945). On this day local festivals are celebrated all over the island.
October 1st	Panca Sila Day ("Day of the Five Principles"), commemorating a speech by President Sukarno (see Famous People) which now forms the preamble of the Indonesian constitution.
October 5th	Armed Forces Day (military parades, etc.).
December 25th/26th	Christmas (western).

Movable holidays

January/February	Chinese New Year (first day of the first Chinese lunar month).
March	Nyepi (see p. 170).
March/April	Ascension (Christian festival) Great birthday (*odalan*) festivals in Pura Besakih and Pura Batur (Kintamani).

Offerings on the beach at Sanur

172

Kite Festival at Padang Galak (near Denpasar).

July

Odalan festival at Pura Kehen, Bangli.

September/
October

Odalan festival at Pura Jagat Natha, Denpasar.

October/
November

Public holidays on Lombok

In contrast to Bali, Lombok has very few festivals, since Islam, the faith dominant on Lombok, has fewer occasions for lively celebrations than the Hinduism of Bali.

Celebrated on the western pattern on December 25th and 31st.

Christmas and
New Year

Celebrated on August 17th, as on Bali.

National Day

Muslim festivals are the Birthday of the Prophet and the end of the fast month of Ramadan.

Movable feasts

Once a year the Sasaks gather in Kuta for a festival during which the legendary Nyale worm is drawn out of the sea.

Other festivals on Lombok are small-scale affairs, confined to the family or the village community. A festival of this kind is held, for example, on the occasion of a girl's first menstruation or a boy's circumcision. The children are carried through the village on wooden animals, the necessary background of noise being provided by drums, pipes and other instruments.

In spite of the cruelty involved cockfighting is a popular sport on Lombok and is the occasion of much betting. The specially trained cocks

Cockfighting

Fighting cocks on Lombok

have razor-sharp blades attached to their legs, and the contest frequently ends only with the death of one of the contestants.

Since the dates of festivals on Bali and Lombok are fixed on the basis of the three different calendars in use on the islands (see Calendars) and vary from year to year, it is not possible to give exact dates in advance. The tourist information offices in Denpasar and Mataram (see Information) issue annual brochures (in English) giving the dates of festivals during the year.

Food and Drink

Indonesian cuisine is very varied and full of surprises. Although it has long established its culinary independence it shows clear evidence of Chinese, Malay and Indian influences.

Food

Rice, vegetables, fish and meat

The mainstay of an Indonesian meal is rice (*nasi putih*, boiled rice; *nasi goreng*, fried rice), always served with fresh vegetables prepared in a variety of ways, fish, seafood and/or roast meat (beef, pork, poultry). Sometimes there are noodles; but potatoes are rarely served: they are unknown in Indonesian cuisine, and appear only on the menu of restaurants serving international cuisine.

Spices

A wide variety of spices (chillies, coriander, caraway, curry powder, ginger, garlic) are used in the preparation of Indonesian dishes, in strengths ranging from mild by way of sweet-sour to very hot indeed. Commonly used is *sambal*, a kind of spice paste made from dried and ground red peppers, tomatoes, chillies, onions, garlic and salt, with vegetable oil as a binder.

Rijsttafel

A famous Indonesian speciality is rijsttafel, a meal consisting of a number of dishes which in the ordinary household is eaten on days of high festival.

The menu begins with a vegetable soup, and the main part of the meal consists of rice accompanied by meat cooked in various ways, vegetables, fish, seafood and eggs, with sauces ranging from hot to sweet-sour. The meal is then rounded off with fruit, nuts, coconut, *krupuk* (see below), etc.

Soups

Baso is made from a highly spiced stock with the addition of rice-flour noodles, vegetables and small pieces of meat, *bubur ayam* is a rice soup with pieces of chicken, *bakmi kuah* a (usually highly spiced) stock with vegetables and noodles, *soto babad* a soup made with beef and vegetables.

When the weather is very hot the meal may consist only of a plateful of *capcay kuah* (cabbage soup).

Main dishes

A good and nourishing main dish is *nasi goreng*, which is simpler to prepare than its exotic name might suggest. Rice which has previously been boiled is fried and served with vegetables, onions steamed in oil and strips of beef or pork, the whole thing being spiced with chopped peppers and chillies. Java has a variant of this called *bahmi goreng* in which noodles are used instead of rice.

Other favourite dishes are *ayam goreng* (fried chicken), *kolo bak* (pork) and *babi kecap* (sucking pig) in sweet-sour sauce.

A tasty Balinese speciality is *babi guling*, a young pig grilled over an open fire and served with rice.

Also very tasty are *bebek betutu* (duck wrapped in banana leaves and

Fresh fish: a staple of the Indonesian menu

cooked very slowly in an underground oven) and *bebek panggang* (grilled duck).

A dish of Chinese origin is *cap cai*, a form of chop suey – meat and vegetables cut into convenient sizes, browned in a pan and served with rice.

Martaban is a kind of pancake stuffed with lamb, onions and spices, folded over and browned on both sides.
Pancakes

Satay is a popular Indonesian dish which is an important element of a rijsttafel and is also eaten as a quick snack: tiny kebabs of beef, lamb and pork grilled on a wooden spit over a charcoal fire and dipped in a spicy peanut sauce.
Satay

A speciality of Indonesian cuisine is *krupuk*: fish or prawns in tapioca flour, fried in oil to a crisp.
Krupuk

Popular desserts are *pisang goreng* (fried banana fritters) and rice custard. *Acar* is a savoury of gherkins, small onions, ginger in sweet-sour sauce and roasted peanuts.
Desserts

Fruit

The artistic presentation of fruit and vegetables is a Balinese speciality, and the kitchen staff in the large hotels includes experts in the art of arranging them in attractive displays.

Visitors from the West are confronted by an overwhelming assortment of tropical fruits, many of them unfamiliar or totally unknown. Many restaurants serve fruit as a dessert, varying according to season. Visitors may also be tempted to buy fruit in the market; if they do, they should be sure to wash it before eating it.

Food and Drink

Bananas   There are bananas (*pisang*) throughout the year; the smaller the banana the sweeter. Bananas soaked in coconut milk and grilled are often served as a dessert.

Coconut   The "meat" of the coconut (*kelapa*) is gouged out of the shell with a narrow spoon.

Durian   The durian, notorious for its unpleasant smell, is regarded by Asians as a great delicacy (April to June).

Grapefruit   Grapefruit, usually with sweet-smelling pink flesh, are fresh throughout the year. They are often eaten with a pinch of salt.

Jackfruit   The sweet, aromatic jackfruit (*nangka*), which may weigh several kilograms, is cut into slices and served on ice (August to September).

Limes   Limes – small round green fruit – are the local alternative to lemons. They are in season all year round.
Lemons must be imported and are therefore expensive.

Lychees   Lychees are not as much grown on Bali as in other parts of Indonesia. The light-coloured flesh of the lychee (which is reddish when ripe) tastes sweet and fresh (May to August).

Mango   Mango (*mangga*) ranks with pineapple as perhaps the favourite fruit of visitors to Bali. When fully ripe (with a yellow skin; does not keep well) it is sweet, juicy and aromatic. The fruit is cut in two and eaten with a spoon (March to June).

Oranges   Indonesian oranges have a thin green skin; when yellow they are particularly sweet.

An artistically arranged platter of fruit

The papaya (pawpaw) is the cheapest of all Asian fruits, in season throughout the year. It is served in hotels for breakfast, cut in half, with a half lemon.

Papaya

Warning: If eaten in quantity, it has a highly laxative effect.

The passion fruit, oval in shape, may be up to 20 cm (8 in.) long and ranges in colour from yellowish-green to dark blue. Sweet-sour in taste and juicy and jelly-like in consistency, it is eaten with a spoon.

Passion fruit

Pineapple (*nanas*) is in season, in several species, from April to July. It is rich in vitamin C and low in calories. Some kinds are eaten lightly cooked, which can have a laxative effect.

Pineapple

Rambutan is a small red fruit covered in soft hairy spines which tastes rather like a lychee.

Rambutan

The rose-apple is often shaped like a pear, with a rust-coloured waxen skin and light-coloured porous flesh; both are edible. It has a rather sourish taste and is usually eaten with sugar and a pinch of salt (January to March).

Rose-apple

Drinks

In the warm climate of Bali it is advisable to drink at least two or three litres of liquid a day. What form this should take is a matter for the individual. One thing is certain, however: it should not be taken in the form of alcohol, the undesirable side effects of which are intensified by tropical heat. The best thirst-quenchers are mineral water, tea and fruit juices.

The Indonesian national drink is tea, drunk either cold (*teh es*) for refreshment or hot (*teh panas*) with a meal.

Tea

Warning: Cold tea is sometimes served with ice cubes. To avoid stomach upsets it is advisable to do without the ice.

Coffee is made in the Turkish fashion and served with the grounds.

Coffee

Pineapple juice (*air jeruk*) and coconut milk (*es kelapa muda*) are particularly refreshing.

Fruit juices

Beer (*bir*) is brewed in Indonesia under licence from German, Dutch and Danish firms and is sold under internationally known brand names. In a bar *bir besar* means a large beer, *bir kecil* a small one. Beer is sold in supermarkets in large and small bottles. It is, by western standards, relatively expensive.

Beer

Rice wine (*brem*) and palm wine (*tuak*), sourish in taste, are drunk in country areas.

Wine

A typical Indonesian drink, with a high percentage of alcohol, is arak, a local type of brandy. It is perhaps better taken as an ingredient of a long drink, with rice wine or lemon juice and honey.

Spirits

All the usual international types of spirits are available in hotels, often at very high prices.

Getting to Bali

The national airline, Garuda Indonesia, operates daily from European and North American airports to Jakarta, with onward connections to Bali. There are direct flights to Bali from Australia and New Zealand, and also a few from Europe. The flight from London Gatwick to Sukarno Hatta Airport, Jakarta, takes 17 hours. The Dutch airline KLM flies six times weekly to Jakarta and Bali from Amsterdam; UTA also has a regular service from Paris; and both have connecting flights from London. Saudia, weekly outward via Jeddah, is good value.

There are also services to Bali from all the major airports in East, South and South-East Asia.

From Java

By rail and ferry

It is possible to travel from Java to Bali by rail and ferry, though at the cost of a considerable expenditure of time. From Jakarta and Yogyakarta there are regular trains to the ferry port of Ketapang (to the north of Banyuwangi) at the east end of Java; the journey takes about 16 hours. From there a car ferry (daily, frequent services; 30–45 minutes) crosses the Bali Strait to Gilimanuk at the western tip of Bali. Since there is no railway on Bali, the journey continues by bus.

To Lombok

By air

Lombok is best approached from Bali. The regional airline Merpati has several flights daily between Ngurah Rai Airport (south-west of Denpasar) on Bali and Mataram Airport on Lombok. The flight takes only about 25 minutes; fares are relatively low.

By sea

There are three ferries daily between Padang Bai (east of Klungkung) on Bali and Lembar (south of Mataram) on Lombok. The crossing takes about 4 hours.

There is a faster crossing (2 hours) by the Mabua Express jumbo ferries between Benoa (south of Denpasar) on Bali and Lembar on Lombok.

Golf

See Sport

Handicrafts

See Shopping

Health Care

A holiday in the tropics calls for certain preparations and for certain modes of behaviour during the holiday if it is to be a positive and rewarding experience. You should consult your doctor before setting out in order to eliminate any health risks. This is particularly important in the case of children and pregnant women.

First aid kit

An adequate first aid kit is of more importance when travelling in Asia than in countries nearer home. On the one hand the risks of infection are greater, and on the other many medicines are not available in Asia or go under different names. It is essential to take with you from home a sufficient quantity of any medicines on which you depend (and also of contraceptives).

Other items which your first aid kit should include are scissors, tweezers, cottonwool, two gauze bandages, a pack of dressings, two packs of adhesive bandages, sticking plaster, a disinfectant and medicines for dealing with a temperature, pain, diarrhoea, constipation, travel sickness, circulatory disorders and infections. Also important are sun cream and a cream protecting the skin against insects.

There are no regulations requiring visitors to Indonesia to have protective inoculations unless they come from an infected zone. Nevertheless it is a wise precaution to be protected against tetanus and poliomyelitis. Immunisation is also recommended against hepatitis A, which is transmitted by unhygienically prepared food or drinks (especially ice); anyone at special risk should have an injection of gamma globulin.

Inoculations

There has recently been a recurrence of malaria in South-East Asia. If you expect to be travelling outside the tourist areas it may be wise to take a prophylactic course of pills.

A certificate of your inoculations, with a note of any allergies and your blood group, should be carried with you.

You must allow your body time to adjust to the climate of the tropics. During the first day or two you should avoid strenuous physical effort and should limit your exposure to the sun. A hat, sun glasses and sun creams are essential items of equipment: remember that Bali is near the Equator!

Adjustment to climate

Caution is required in air-conditioned accommodation. Although the coolness is agreeable after the high outdoor temperatures, there is a danger of catching a chill if you spend too long in air-conditioned (that is, usually over-cooled) rooms. The air-conditioning should be turned down at night.

Bali is notorious for the mysterious "Bali fever", in which the temperature suddenly rises to over 39°C (102°F), as a rule without any other symptoms. It is usually cured by a fever-reducing drug and a couple of days in bed. If it persists a doctor should be consulted.

Bali fever

It is usually quite safe to eat at a hot food stall

Help for the Disabled

AIDS	The danger of contracting AIDS is relatively high in Indonesia. The usual precautions should be taken: the use of condoms in either heterosexual or homosexual intercourse and of one-time syringes for any injections, with caution when undergoing blood transfusions, surgical operations or dental treatment.
Diet	Although eating at hot food stalls usually does westerners no harm, you should check on the cleanliness of a stall before deciding to patronise it. All fruit should be thoroughly washed before being eaten. You should avoid eating uncooked food, unpeeled fruit, ices and non-bottled drinks, which are usually served with ice-cubes. Moderation in the drinking of alcohol is advisable, since heat intensifies its effects.
During the flight	During a long flight light-weight, comfortable clothing is best; veteran air travellers swear by a pair of comfortable slippers. An inflatable cushion, of the type resembling a ruff, is useful for supporting the head while sleeping.
Cleanliness	The best protection against infection is meticulous cleanliness (frequent washing of the hands, showering, change of clothing).

Help for the Disabled

General information	In Britain the main sources of information and advice on travel by the disabled are the Royal Association for Disability and Rehabilitation (RADAR), 12 City Forum, 250 City Road, London EC1V 8AF, tel. (0171) 2503222; the Spinal Injuries Association, 76 St James Lane, London N10 3DS, tel. (0181) 4442121; and Mobility International, 228 Borough High Street, London SE1 1JX, tel. (0171) 4035688. Major sources of information in the United States are Louise Weiss's "Access to the World: A Travel Guide for the Handicapped" (available from Facts on File, 460 Park Avenue South, New York NY 10016) and the Society for the Advancement of Travel by the Handicapped, 26 Court Street, Penthouse Suite, Brooklyn NY 11242.
Useful publications	"Holiday and Travel Abroad – A Guide for Disabled People", published by RADAR. "The World Wheelchair Traveller", published by the AA for the Spinal Injuries Association. "Low Cost Travel Tips for People Using Wheelchairs", published by Mobility International. The AA also publishes a "Guide for the Disabled Traveller" (free to members).
Transport on Bali	It is exceptional to find facilities for the disabled on public transport on Bali; but disabled persons can rely on getting help from local people.
Sightseeing	Most sights on Bali, particularly temples, can be visited in wheelchairs.
Hotels	The larger hotels in particular cater to some extent for the needs of disabled people. No list of such hotels, however, is available.

Hotels

On Bali	The hotels on Bali are quite up to international standards. Many of the international hotel chains are represented here, together with innumerable local operators. Naturally, it is considerably cheaper to stay in the many small hotels which offer relatively modest comfort but

compensate for this by paying careful attention to their guests. The hotels called "Homestay" or "Losmen" offer the best value for money and can be found in almost every locality on Bali.

Formerly, Lombok Island to the east of Bali was only a place for excursions and offered modest accommodation. However, a few years ago Bali's neighbouring island was discovered by the tourist industry and several comfortable hotels were built, mainly on Sengiggi Beach north of the capital Mataram.

On Lombok

A list of hotels is available from the Indonesian Tourist Board (see information).

It is essential, particularly during the main holiday season (April–October), to book well in advance. It is almost impossible to find accommodation before and after Ramadan, the Muslim month of fasting, since many visitors from neighbouring Muslim countries take their holiday here at these times.

Reservation

Hotels on Bali

Balina Beach, tel. 91368, fax 92579. This beautiful small hotel with only 20 bungalows stands on a quiet inlet a short distance from Candi Dasa and therefore also from the tourist bustle. There are bicycles for hire.

Candi Dasa

★Puri Bagus Beach Hotel, tel. 751223, fax 752779, 30 rooms. This relatively new bungalow complex stands at the eastern end of Candi Dasa (in the direction of Amlapura). It is particularly good for water-sports enthusiasts visiting Bali (snorkelling equipment, surf boards and sailing boats are available for hire; diving school under German management).

★Pamecutan Palace, Jalan Thamrin 2, tel. 223491. The contrast could hardly be greater: outside the walls which surround the former princely palace, the Puri Pamecutan, the traffic of the capital roars – on the inside cocks in willow baskets occasionally engage in a crowing competition.

Denpasar

Sua Bali (on the road from Denpasar to Gianyar near Blahbatuh), tel. 361941050, fax 361941035. Not so much a hotel, more accommodation in which visitors to Bali can experience socially compatible tourism at close quarters. It stands in a fascinating landscape at the edge of the village of Kemenuh. Here it is easy to live and eat like the Balinese and to make contacts with the locals.

Gianyar

★Four Seasons Resort, tel. 771288, fax. 771280, 139 rooms. Truly the best hotel on Bali with stylish and luxuriously furnished bungalows set in the middle of a tropical landscape. The distinguishing feature: each bungalow resembles an independent Balinese farmstead, even the family altar has not been forgotten. Each bungalow has its own small pool.

Jimbaran

★Amankila, tel. 221993, fax 221995, 35 bungalows. Mick Jagger of the Rolling Stones looks in from time to time and stays for a few days in the luxurious bungalow which – according to credible reports – is reserved just for him throughout the whole year. In order to bump into him on the odd occasion requires a lot of money. However, in return for the truly high room prices you get the very best which Bali has to offer.

Klungkung

★Puri Anyar (former princely palace), tel. 223602, 12 rooms. Anyone who can do without a swimming pool and night club will find the very best accommodation in the former palace, the Puri Anyar. The subtropical gardens are a sight in themselves.

Krambitan

The palace of Puri Anyar in Krambitan, now a hotel

Kuta/Legian

★Kartika Plaza, Jalan Kartika, tel. 751067–9, fax 752475, 400 rooms. A very extensive hotel with an enormous park, several pools and excellent restaurants. Hotel guests and others like to meet in the basement night club where there is live music.

★Bali Oberoi, Jalan Kayu Aya, tel. 751061, fax 752791, 60 rooms. One the very best addresses on Bali; which is also reflected in the price. However, if you like style and atmosphere then this is the place for you.

★Seminyak Ramah Village, Gang Keraton, tel. 730793 fax 730793, 16 bungalows. The variously sized bungalows are furnished in the local style and can be reserved for really acceptable prices (from £14). The owner has created a dream in the luxurious subtropical landscape and now passes it on to others.

Lovina

Lovina Beach lies on the northern side of Bali. Since this region was only developed for tourism a few years ago, individual hotels or guest houses will not be recommended in this guide. As a rule they do not achieve the high standards of the hotels on the south coast. Nevertheless, they are an alternative for those who are looking for quiet accommodation away from the rush. There are several hotels and guest houses along the coast road from Singaraja to Pengastulan. Generally, the prices are more favourable than in the south of the island.

Nusa Dua

Bali Sol, tel. 771510, fax 772148, 500 rooms. An extensive hotel at Nusa Dua point with large but sensibly furnished rooms. Apart from the hotel's own beach there is one of the largest swimming pools on Bali, also fitness and sauna equipment as well as a diving base.

Nusa Dua Beach Hotel, tel. 771210, fax 771229, 450 rooms. Judged by the number of its rooms this is one of the largest hotels on Bali. Its clever incorporation into the landscape hides this fact. Here the holiday maker can find everything from swimming pool to discotheque.

★Sheraton Lagoon Nusa Dua, tel. 771801, fax 771323, 275 rooms. The Bali Sheraton is certainly one of the very best addresses in this world-wide hotel chain. Expensive, lavish and excellent.

★Matahari Beach Resort, tel. 36292312, fax 92313, 16 bungalows. The Bali Barat National Park lies right on the doorstep which is ideal for naturalists. Diving trips to Menjangan island are possible and also mountain bike tours. The hotel is owned by a Bavarian and the head chef comes from Austria.

Pemuteran

Grand Bali Beach, Jalan Raya Sanur, tel. 288511, fax 287917, 650 rooms. One should be grateful to the builder of this facility for the simple reason that he erected a high-rise building which, at the time, even frightened the government in Denpasar who decreed that no new hotel should be higher than the tallest palm tree in the area. To date builders have kept to this ruling and the Grand Bali Beach is simply an example of the building style in the "old" days. But time heals many wounds; even those which were inflicted upon the attractive countryside by this quite comfortable hotel.

Sanur

Sanur Beach Hotel, Jalan Semawang, tel. 2880511–5, fax 287566, 321 rooms. The Balinese style is here complemented quite well by the design requirements of a purpose-built hotel. The Prahu Lounge is an original concept; a fishing boat converted into a small restaurant.

★Ubud Villa Cempaka, Jalan Bisma, tel. 96312, fax 96312, 10 bungalows. This small hotel, with bungalows and acceptable prices, stands in extensive grounds which are mostly left to nature.

Ubud

The Matahari Beach Resort hotel: the place for lovers of nature.

Hotels on Lombok

Chakranegara   Ratih Hotel, 127 Jalan Panjanggik, tel. (0364) 21096, 41 rooms. A centrally positioned hotel with comfortable bungalows in carefully designed surroundings.

Sengiggi Beach   ★The Oberoi Lombok, tel. (0364) 38444, fax 32496, 50 villas. One of the most beautiful and sophisticated houses in the well-known hotel chain which was only opened in 1998. Wonderful subtropical surroundings with every comfort; ideal for water sport activities.

★Sengiggi Beach Hotel, tel. (0364) 93210, fax 93200, 150 rooms. Extensive buildings with comfortable bungalows under tall palm trees. There are numerous opportunities for sports enthusiasts: diving, snorkelling, tennis, badminton, table tennis, wind-surfing.

Sheraton Sengiggi Beach Resort, tel. (0364) 93333, fax 93140, 158 rooms. One of the most expensive hotels on Lombok but for this you receive many benefits. The hotel complex bears the signature of local artists who drew on the folkcraft of the island's inhabitants in the design.

Illness

Health services   Adequate medical care is available on Bali and Lombok, particularly in the tourist centres. In towns and villages all over the islands there are doctors in private practice, though few of them have any great knowledge of English.

Medical Aid

Doctors   The large hotels can call on English-speaking doctors, who will be summoned by reception in case of need. In case of emergency the local representative of the tour operator with whom the visitor is travelling can get a suitable doctor or dentist.

Ambulance   The ambulance service on Bali and Lombok is, by western standards, poor, and in the event of an accident outside the tourist areas there may be a long wait for an ambulance. As a rule, however, you can always rely on the ready helpfulness of the Balinese.

Air ambulance   If it becomes necessary on medical grounds to fly a patient home, an air ambulance must be ordered in his home country. Alternatively – though only in the case of non-life-threatening illness or injury – it may be possible to arrange for an ordinary aircraft to be used by removing a number of seats to make room for a stretcher.
In case of need the appropriate airline (see Air Services) should be approached; or the patient's consulate or embassy (see Embassies and Consulates) may be able to help.
Since either of these methods of transport will be very expensive, it is highly desirable, before leaving home, to take out insurance covering return home by air when required on medical grounds.

Hospitals

There are no hospitals on Bali equipped for treating severe injuries or life-threatening diseases. In such cases, therefore, transfer of the patient to Jakarta or Singapore must be considered. The patient's consulate or embassy should also be informed.

Primary treatment can, however, be obtained in the following hospitals:

Army Hospital, Jalan Panglima Sudirman, Denpasar
Tel. 228003

Dharma Usaha Hospital, Jalan Panglima Sudirman, Denpasar
Tel. 975235

Kasih Ibu, Jalan Teuku Umar 120, Denpasar
Tel. 223036 and 237016

Manuaba Hospital, Jalan H. O. S. Cokroaminoto 28, Denpasar
Tel. 2426393

Hospitals with
24-hour
outpatient
departments

Kuta Clinic, Jalan Raya Kuta 100 X, Kuta
Tel. 753268

Nusa Dua Clinic, Jalan Pratama 81 A–B, Nusa Dua
Tel. 771324

Information

Great Britain

Indonesian Tourist Board
3–4 Hanover Street
London W19 HH
Tel. (0171) 4930030

This office also covers Ireland, Benelux and Scandinavia. Information may also be obtained from the airline Garuda Indonesia (see Air Services, Airlines), the Indonesian Embassy (see Embassies and Consulates) or Indonesian Express Travel Agent, 70 New Bond Street, London W1Y 9DE, tel. (0171) 4914469.

In Europe

Indonesia Tourist Promotion Offices
Wiesenhüttenstrasse 17
D–6000 Frankfurt am Main
Germany
Tel. (0611) 233677

The Frankfurt office covers the rest of Europe.

In North America and Australasia

Indonesia Tourist Promotion Offices
3457 Wilshire Boulevard
Los Angeles CA 90010
Tel. (213) 3872078

United States

Indonesia Tourist Promotion Offices
Level 10, 5 Elizabeth Street
Sydney 2000
Tel. (02) 2333630

Australia

On Bali

Denpasar

Bali Government Tourist Office
Kompleks Niti Mandala
Jalan S. Parman
Tel. 222387 and 226313
Open Mon.–Thu. 7.30am–2.30pm, Fri. 7.30–11.30am,
Sat. 7.30am–12.30pm

Badung Government Tourist Office
Jalan Surapati 7
Tel. 223399 and 223602
Open Mon.–Thu. 8am–2pm, Fri. 8–11am,
Sat. 8am–12.30pm

Kuta

Kuta Government Tourist Office
Jalan Bakung Sari / Jalan Raya Kuta
Tel. 751419
Open Mon.–Sat. 8am–3pm

Ubud

In Ubud there is a privately run information office, Bina Wisata, Jalan
Raya (open Mon.–Sat. 8.30am–7.30pm), which produces a good general
map of the area showing the main sights and can supply information
about the times of temple festivals and other events.

On Lombok

Lombok Regional Tourism Office
Jalan Indrakila 2 A
Mataram
Tel. (0364) 22327 and 22723
Open Mon.–Sat. 8am–5pm

Language

Bahasa Indonesia

Unlike many other Asian languages, Bahasa Indonesia (Bahasa for
short), the national language of Indonesia, which is closely related to the
Malay language, is relatively easy for Westerners to learn: there are, for
example, no varying tones as in Chinese.

Grammar

The grammar of the Malay language is simpler than that of European
languages. There are, for example, few plural forms: the plural is often
expressed merely by doubling the singular (*bulan* = "month"; *bulan-
bulan* = "months"). (A doubled word can also, in certain circumstances,
take on a quite different meaning.)

Bahasa Indonesia has no articles. The sentence "What is the price of
the room?" is in Bahasa "Berapa harga kamar kosong ini?" ("What costs
room?").

The verb is not conjugated: the mood or tense is deduced from the
meaning of the sentence. Possessive pronouns come after the thing pos-
sessed. "My room" is *kamarku* (-*ku* = "my").

Pronunciation

Spelling is phonetic. Vowels are pronounced as in Italian, for example;
i.e. without diphthongisation as in English. Most consonants are as in
English: exceptions are c (pronounced ch) and z (pronounced ts).

Stress

The stress in a word is almost always on the penultimate syllable. In a
sentence the most important word is stressed: e.g. in *selamat pagi!*
("good morning!") the stress is on the second word ("morning").

Formal forms of address are not usual in Indonesia, and there are no standard phrases for the purpose. Conversations tend to begin with general topics.

A favourite way of opening a conversation is to ask the other person's name ("Siapa namayana?") or where he comes from. Sometimes, as in English, the question is asked, "How are you?" ("Apa khabar?"), to which the answer is either "Bagus, bagus" ("Well, well") or "Khabar baik" ("I feel well").

Indonesia is mainly a Muslim country, and accordingly a few Arabic words have found their way into the language: e.g. "Selamat!" ("May your deeds be blessed!"), which is always used in conjunction with a time of day or a wish of some kind. For example:

Selamat datang!	Welcome!
Selamat jalan!	Bon voyage!
Selamat pagi!	Good morning!
Selamat siang!	Good day!
Selamat sore!	Good afternoon!
Selamat malam!	Good night!
Selamat tinggal!	Goodbye!
Selamat makan!	Bon appétit!

Useful words and expressions

English	**Indonesian**	
Yes	Ya/tentu	
No	Tidak/bukan	
Please	Silakan/tolong	
Thank you	Terimah kasih	
Please help me!	Tolonglah saya!	
Not at all	Kembali	
Excuse me	Ma'af	
What time is it?	Jam berapa?	
No, I don't want to	Tidak mau	
I do not speak Indonesian	Saya tidak mengerti bahasa	
I do not understand	Saya tidak mengerti	
What does that cost?	Berapa harga ini?	
That is too dear	Ini terlalu mahal	
The bill, please!	Totong bonnya!	
Aircraft	Kapal terbang	Transport
Airport	Airport, bandar udara	
Automobile, car	Mobil	
Bicycle	Sepeda	
Boat, ship	Kapal laut	
Bus	Bis	
Bus station	Bis setasiun	
Fast	Cepat	
Horse-drawn carriage	Dokar (Lombok) Cidomo	
Lane	Gang	
Left	Kiri	
Motorcycle	Sepeda motor	
Railway station	Setasiun	
Right	Kanan	
Slow	Pelan (pelan-pelan)	
Straight ahead	Terus	
Street	Jalan	
Taxi	Taksi	
What is the name of this street?	Nama saudara jalan?	

Language

	English	**Indonesian**
Accommodation	Hotel	Hotel
	(Other forms of accommodation)	Homestay, losmen
	Have you a room?	Masih ada kamar kosong disini?
	What is the price of the room?	Berapa harga untuk kamar ini?
Geographical terms	Beach	Pantai
	Hill	Bukit
	Hot spring	Air panas
	Island	Pulau, nusa
	Mountain	Gunung
	Peak, summit	Puncak
	River	Sungai
	Town	Kampong
	Village	Desa
	Volcano	Gunung api
	Waterfall	Air terjun
Days of week	Sunday	Minggu
	Monday	Senin
	Tuesday	Selasa
	Wednesday	Rabu
	Thursday	Kamis
	Friday	Jum'at
	Saturday	Sabtu
Months	January	Januari
	February	Februari
	March	Maret
	April	April
	May	Mei
	June	Juni
	July	Juli
	August	Agustus
	September	September
	October	Oktober
	November	November
	December	Desember
Time	Day	Hari
	Week	Minggu
	Month	Bulan
	Year	Tahun
Times of day	Morning	Pahi hari
	Noon	Siang
	Evening	Malam
	Night	Malam hari
	Yesterday	Kemarin
	Today	Hara ini
	Tomorrow	Besok
	Day after tomorrow	Besok lusa

Numbers

0 nol	17 tujuhbelas
1 satu	18 delapanbelas
2 dua	19 sembilanbelas
3 tiga	20 dua puluh
4 empat	21 dua puluh satu
5 lima	22 dua puluh dua
6 enam	23 dua puluh tiga
7 tujuh	30 tiga puluh
8 delapan	50 lima puluh

9	sembilan	100	seratus
10	sepuluh	200	dua ratus
11	sebelas	500	lima ratus
12	duabelas	1000	seribu
13	tigabelas	10,000	sepuluh ribu
14	empatbelas	100,000	seratus ribu
15	limabelas	1,000,000	sejuta
16	enambelas		

See entry

Food and drink

Lost Property

See Safety

Markets

All over Bali and Lombok lively and colourful markets are held daily. Their primary purpose is to sell the agricultural produce of the area, but they also offer visitors picturesque subjects for their cameras and camcorders. Before taking any photographs, however, you should make sure that those who will appear in them have no objection.

The best time to visit a market is in the morning, preferably early in the morning.

Beware of light-fingered pickpockets!

A market on Bali and ...   *... on Lombok*

Medical Aid

See Emergencies, Illness

Motorcycle Rental

See Car Rental

Motoring

Asian drivers have a rather different attitude to motor vehicles and to driving them from that of westerners, and the people of Bali and Lombok are no exception. Putting it perhaps rather crudely, it can be said that a driver here proceeds on the very simple principle that the five drivers in front of him, the five others behind him and the seventeen cyclists, motorcyclists and pedestrians to right and left will behave exactly as they ought and do nothing silly. Traffic regulations are more honoured in the breach than in the observance, and speed limits seem to be regarded as a challenge to get the last ounce of speed out of vehicles which are often barely roadworthy. It will be understood, therefore, that extreme caution is called for in driving on Bali or Lombok.

Rule of the road
In Indonesia, including Bali and Lombok, vehicles travel on the left, with overtaking on the right.

Roads
With the exception of the four-lane Jalan Bypass between Denpasar and Nusa Dua there are no motorways or expressways on Bali. In country areas in particular the condition of even important trunk roads is extremely precarious. Potholes, corrugated surfaces and soft verges can crop up without warning: additional arguments in favour of slow and careful driving. Local drivers make generous use of their horns, particularly in built-up area, and this is a practice which visitors soon learn to follow.

Road signs
With some exceptions, road signs are in line with international standards. There is no systematic road numbering on Bali, and road numbers are not shown on road maps.

Speed limits
Speed limits – even though few local drivers observe them – are 40 km (25 mi.) an hour in built-up areas and 80 km (50 mi.) an hour for cars and 50 km (31 mi.) an hour for buses and lorries on the open road.

Car rental
See entry

Breakdown assistance

On Bali there are no road patrols by motoring organisations and no emergency telephones along the roads. Motorists in trouble are therefore dependent on other road users for assistance. If you have a breakdown you should attract the attention of any vehicles that come along; and since the Balinese like to be helpful you will probably not have to wait long. If the fault cannot be put right on the spot the other driver will usually be ready to take you to the nearest garage to get any necessary spare part. Towing to a garage by another vehicle is permitted.

A breakdown at night may be more of a problem, particularly outside the tourist areas, since you may have to wait a long time for assistance. This is a good reason for avoiding night driving.

When you hire a car you ought to be given a list of reliable garages. If no such list is available you should ask for advice on what to do in the event of a breakdown.

Repair garages

Bali is relatively well provided with petrol stations (which are never self-service). Before filling up you should check that the petrol is right for your vehicle. Pumps are usually labelled in English as well as in Indonesian.

Petrol stations

Museums

Bali has a number of interesting museums which are well worth a visit. The Bali National Museum in Denpasar (see entry) is of interest to every visitor to Bali. It offers an excellent introduction to the history of the island, with a fine collection of exhibits of cultural and religious interest (costumes, weapons, cult objects, etc.). There are dioramas showing important events in the life of the Balinese, like the ceremonies of tooth-filing and cremation.

On Bali

A small museum in Tabanan (see entry) illustrates the history of rice-growing on Bali, with examples of the implements used by the rice-farmers.

There is an archaeological museum in Bedulu (see entry).

Balinese painting is world-famed, and Ubud (see entry), the "city of artists", has two galleries showing important works by painters working on Bali, the Neka Museum and Antonio Blanco's studio. The Agung Rai Gallery in Peliatan (see entry) is another interesting collection. The Werdi Budaya Art Centre in Denpasar (see entry) has a permanent exhibition of Balinese painting, and the Le Mayeur House in Sanur has a collection of work by the Belgian artist of that name.

In the Bali National Museum

191

The village of Penglipuran: almost an open-air museum

Visitors interested in Balinese history will want to visit the Gedong Kirtya Library in Singaraja with its collection of valuable lontar (palm-leaf) manuscripts.

The little village of Penglipuran near Bangli is a kind of open-air museum in itself.

On Lombok

The chief town of Lombok, Mataram, has an interesting museum, mainly devoted to the history of the Sasaks, the indigenous inhabitants of the island.

Newspapers and Periodicals

There are more than 70 daily newspapers published in Indonesia, including three in English – the "Jakarta Post", the "Indonesian Observer" and the "Indonesian Times" – which are obtainable throughout the country. The English-language "Bali Post" appears twice monthly.

Although there is no direct censorship, there are numerous laws on the press which prevent the publication of material critical of the government.

Western newspapers and periodicals are obtainable only in the large hotels, and are very expensive.

Night Life

Night life as it is understood in the West appeared on Bali only when foreign visitors began to flock to the island, and it is still confined to the main tourist areas.

The island's principal entertainment centre, with bars, discos and other attractions, is Kuta Beach, which has now joined up with the neighbouring township of Legian. All the large hotels in Nusa Dua, on the Bukit Badung peninsula in southern Bali, have their own night spots. In Sanur night life is on a relatively modest scale, and there too it is centred on the hotels.

The centre of night life in Kuta/Legian is the area bounded by Jalan Pantai Kuta and Jalan Legian. In this quarter are numerous "in" places (e.g. "Goa" and "Yummie"), mainly patronised by the younger set. Many bars, such as the Jaya Pub and Cafç Luna in Jalan Legian and the Tavern in the Kartika Plaza Beach Hotel, have live music. There are numerous discos, some of them charging for admission or requiring a minimum expenditure on drinks.

The Strand Bar (under German management) in Jalan Double Six has become an artists' rendezvous, with temporary exhibitions of work by both Balinese and visiting artists.

Opening Times

See Business Hours

Photography

The Indonesian archipelago, particularly Bali, is one of the most photogenic areas in the world. Photographers should be sure, therefore, to bring plenty of film with them: films bought locally are expensive and have not always been properly stored.

The best times for photography are in the morning and afternoon, when the sun is not too high in the sky. Skylight and polarising filters are essential. Salt water and salty air are harmful to cameras and lenses, and special cleaning substances and cloths should be part of the photographer's equipment. The lens should always be covered when not in use.

As a rule the Balinese like to be photographed; but before taking a photograph you should always ask permission (a gesture with the camera is usually sufficient) and not insist if it is refused: a person who does not want to be photographed will not be persuaded by the offer of money. Strict Hindus are sometimes camera-shy. It goes without saying that you should not take a close-up photograph of people practising their religion; in such circumstances experienced photographers use a long-focus lens.

At many temple festivals it is strictly forbidden to use flash; the alternative is to use high-speed film. The Balinese object strongly to visitors using sacred objects as background or props for their holiday snaps. Climbing on temple walls or on temple figures is also strictly prohibited, and offenders are liable to heavy fines. To the Balinese this is not merely a criminal offence: it is a desecration of the temple, which must then be cleansed by elaborate rites (see Social Conduct).

If you promise to send someone a print of your photograph you must be sure to keep your promise: not to do so involves a loss of face, which in Asia is a very serious matter.

In the tourist centres there are numerous laboratories for the rapid development of film, which usually do a good job at reasonable prices. Transparencies are better kept for development at home.

The X-ray machines for the examination of baggage (both hand baggage and checked-in baggage) are not always guaranteed to avoid damage to films. All film, both exposed and unexposed, should be

The Balinese are cheerful people and ...   *... usually not at all camera-shy*

carried in your hand baggage, and if there is any doubt about the safety of your film (particularly fast film) you should insist on having it checked without passing through the machine.

Postal and Telephone Services

Postal services on Bali and Lombok are usually reliable. Letters and postcards to Europe normally take between seven and ten days by air mail.

Post offices in Denpasar | The Central Post Office in Denpasar is in Jalan Raya Pupatan. There are other post offices in Sanur (Jalan Buyan), Kuta (Jalan Raya Tuban) and Ubud (Jalan Jembawan, opposite the Neka Gallery).

Opening times | Mon.–Thu. 8am–2pm, Fri. 8am–11am, Sat. 8am–12.30pm.

Post-boxes | Indonesian post-boxes are red. Collection times are shown in a panel on the front.

Hotels | Mail can be handed in at the reception desk of your hotel, which can be relied on to send it on its way.

Rates | The postage on a letter to Europe (air mail) is 1600 rupiahs, on a postcard 1200 rupiahs. For safety's sake important letters should be registered.
Postage on packets and parcels varies according to weight. The postage on a particular item can be ascertained by enquiry at the Central Post Office in Denpasar or at the reception desk of your hotel.

Children telephoning and ...   *... a post-box on Bali*

Indonesian stamps, with their varied and often very attractive designs, make good souvenirs, particularly of course for stamp-collectors. Post offices and drugstores in hotels usually have a selection, both mint and used.

Stamps

Telephoning on Bali and Lombok can sometimes be a lengthy and frustrating process, since the system is often overloaded.

There are coin-operated payphones, but card-operated telephones are now more common. Telephone cards can be bought at post offices.

Telephoning

Many large hotels have international direct dialling (IDD; expensive); otherwise it is necessary to go through the operator. It is also possible to make international calls from all post offices, though long waits must be expected. Ordinary overseas telephone calls are somewhat cheaper (as is the sending of faxes) via Wartel Telecommunications (see below).

International calls

A 3-minute call to Europe by satellite costs about 28,000 rupiahs. Local calls from public telephones cost 50 rupiahs (more from hotels).

Telephone charges

From the United Kingdom
to Indonesia 0010 62
to Bali 0010 62361
to Lombok 0010 62364

International dialling codes

From the United States and Canada
to Indonesia 011 62
to Bali 011 62361
to Lombok 011 62364

From Bali and Lombok
to the United Kingdom 00 44
to the United States or Canada 00 1

195

For IDD calls there may sometimes be special codes, which will be shown in a leaflet in your hotel room.

Local dialling

On Bali there are no local dialling codes: the first figure of a telephone number identifies the area.

Telephone enquiries

Domestic: dial 100. International: dial 101.

Telegrams

Telegrams are accepted at most post offices. A telegram to Europe will reach its destination in about a day.

Fax

Faxes can be sent from the offices of Wartel Telecommunications in all the larger towns, which are identified by white signs with black lettering and a blue emblem (telephone charges are cheaper there too).

Almost all hotels now have fax machines, which can be used by residents and sometimes by non-residents. There may be a minimum charge (usually about the cost of a 3-minute telephone call).

Business centres

The larger hotels have business centres providing business travellers with all modern communications facilities.

Public Transport

Taxis

There are something like 400 taxis with taximeters in Denpasar, identified by their blue and yellow paintwork. There are also large numbers of "rogue" taxis without meters; before hiring one of these it is necessary to settle the fare by a process of bargaining. During the day and in the early evening the meters in the regular taxis are usually switched on;

Balinese School children get in a Bemo

but later in the evening and at weekends, when taxis tend to be in short supply, the driver often states a fare, which you can either accept – or try to get a better price from the next taxi to come along. For longer journeys the drivers are usually ready to negotiate a fixed fare.

A journey by bus on Bali can be, in its own way, a memorable experience. For the Balinese it is the cheapest form of transport for both short and long distances. Fares are fixed and not subject to bargaining. There are no timetables: the driver of the bus usually waits at the bus station until he has enough passengers to make the journey worth his while.

Buses

A very common form of transport is the bemo, originally a pickup truck lined with benches but now generally a minibus. A bemo is convenient for short journeys but less comfortable than a bus for longer ones.

Bemos

The name colt comes from the Mitsubishi Colt, but is now commonly applied to any minibus.

Colts

A dokar (called a cidomo on Lombok) is a pony trap, a two-wheeled carriage drawn by a single horse. A trip in a dokar is (except in Denpasar) an agreeable and tranquil experience. It is the local people's favourite means of transport for short distances. The fare, which will be modest, must be negotiated before setting out.

Dokars, cidomos

A certain amount of courage is necessary to entrust yourself to one of the increasingly common ojeks (motorcycle taxis). The drivers have at any rate the experience and skill required to cope with Balinese traffic conditions, though many of them confuse the island's roads with a racetrack. In addition to negotiating the fare in advance you should ask for a crash helmet.

Ojeks

A cidomo on Lombok

Radio and Television

Car rental	See entry
Boat rental	See Boat Charter
Ferries	See Ferry Services

Radio and Television

Radio in English	A radio station on Bali transmits English-language news bulletins every hour on the hour. The BBC World Service, the Voice of America and Radio Australia can be picked up on short wave.
Television	The government television service, based in Jakarta, transmits programmes in Bahasa Indonesia which can be received on Bali.

Religious Services

Protestant	Maranatha Church Jalan Surapati, Denpasar Eklesia Church Raya Tuban, Kuta Services: Sunday at 9am and 6pm At the Bali Beach Inter-Continental Hotel in Sanur there is a Protestant service every Sunday at 6.30pm
Roman Catholic	Catholic Church Jalan Kepundung, Denpasar Services: Sunday at 7am, 8.30am and 5.30pm Church of St Francis Xavier Jalan Kartika Plaza, Kuta Services: Saturday at 6pm and Sunday at 8am In addition, Catholic Masses are held in the Bali Beach Inter-Continental Hotel (Legong Room) Sanur on Saturday at 6pm and in the Bali Hyatt Hotel (Hibiscus Room) on Saturday at 7pm and also in the Meliá Bali Sol Hotel Nusa Dua on Sunday at 6am
Mosque	There is an Islamic Mosque in the Jalan Hassanuddin, Denpasar which is also open to Muslims of other nations.

Restaurants

Alongside the Indonesian cuisine (*rumah makan*) which is served in innumerable restaurants the standard international cuisine has now established itself on Bali and Lombok, particularly in the areas frequented by tourists. Whether a Wiener Schnitzel tastes the same in Indonesia as in Vienna may be questioned; but in any case Indonesian food is so good and so varied that one can manage very well without European dishes. See Food and Drink.

Reservation	In the better-class restaurants it is advisable to book a table in advance. It is usual, on entering a restaurant, to wait for a waiter to show you to your table.

A roadside warung makan

See entry   Tipping

The hot food stalls found in many Asian countries are known on Bali as   Hot food stalls
warungs. A *warung makan* is a modest restaurant open to the street in
which simple dishes, particularly soups, are served. In general visitors
need have no hesitation in eating in a *warung makan*.

In view of the large numbers of restaurants of all kinds no attempt is
made to list them here. Visitors will usually be able to make their own
discoveries; otherwise the best plan is to ask at the hotel reception desk.

River Rafting

River rafting is possible on the river Ayung. From the starting-point at
the village of Kedewatan, below Bedugul, there is a run of 11 km (7 mi.)
to just above Ubud. The trip (which is not particularly cheap) is made in
rubber dinghies steered by experienced guides. Those interested in this
sport can apply to:

P. T. Bali Adventure Rafting
Jalan Tunjung Mekar, Legian
Tel. 751292 or 262316

Sobek Expeditions
Jalan Bypass Ngurah Rai 56 X, Sanur
Tel. 287059

Preparing for a river rafting trip

Safety

In terms of safety and security Bali is no "Island of the Blessed"; but its crime rate is no higher than that of other tourist regions of the world. Remembering that "the occasion makes the thief", visitors should take appropriate precautions. It should be borne in mind that a holidaymaker on Bali will often be carrying more money on him than a lowly hotel employee earns in a month: he should, therefore, keep a careful eye on his possessions, avoid making a display of his higher standard of living and leave valuables in the hotel safe; and he should never carry more money than he expects to spend.

Room keys should always be left at the hotel reception desk.

Safes

Most of the large hotels have safe-deposit boxes and sometimes room safes, in which visitors should deposit money and valuables. If this is not done hotels accept no responsibility for loss by theft.

On the beach

You should take no valuables or large sums of money with you to the beach.

Travel documents

You should make photocopies of travel documents (passports and other identity papers, tickets, etc.) before leaving home and carry the copies separately from the originals. This will facilitate their replacement if they are lost.

Travellers' cheques

The receipt for travellers' cheques, and a note of their numbers, should be kept separately from the cheques themselves. This will enable them to be replaced if they are lost or stolen.

See Currency

You should keep a note of important telephone numbers – your bank, the agencies who issued your credit cards and travellers' cheques, etc.

Beware of pickpockets, particularly in markets and in large crowds. Money and other valuables should be carried in an inside pocket or in a special belt not visible from outside.

There are no lost property offices in Indonesia. Lost property is handed in – if at all – at a police station (see Emergencies).
Indonesians are, in general, honest; but, as in other countries, there are exceptions to the rule.

See entry

Shopping

Bali is not a shoppers' paradise like Singapore, Bangkok or Hong Kong, but the Balinese are famed for their skill in producing attractive hand-crafted articles.

Visitors do not have to look far for typical local products to take home. All the larger hotels have their own souvenir shops, and in the areas frequented by tourists there are swarms of street traders as well as shops and stalls selling a variety of souvenirs. Outside the tourist areas and in the interior of the island prices are usually lower.

Except in established shops and hotels bargaining is the rule: to Asians haggling over the price of a purchase is a kind of national sport.

The following selection suggests typical souvenirs and the best place to buy them.

The village of Mas, near Ubud, is one of the main centres of artistic woodcarving (masks worn in dances, figures, etc.). Here you can buy them, as it were, direct from the factory, and at correspondingly lower prices. There are also good woodcarvers in the neighbouring village of Nyuhkuning.

Ubud is the recognised art centre of the island, with numerous painters whose work is displayed in many shops in the town. Balinese paintings can also be bought in Pengosekan, 3 km (2 mi.) south of Ubud.

Batik work can be bought all over Bali. Not all the material sold as batik, however, is genuine: much of it is machine- or screen-printed in factories.

Genuine ikat fabrics are expensive, since ikat is a time-consuming process which must be done by hand (see p. 56). Double ikat fabrics can be found only in Tenganan.

Bali has developed a considerable industry catering for the requirements of visitors. Sport and leisure clothing, T-shirts and other items of clothing and accessories can be bought here at distinctly lower prices than in the West. It is advisable, however, to check the quality of anything you buy.

The gold jewellery produced on Bali (almost always 14 carats) has a strong yellow colour.

Balinese silverware is of high quality. The best places to look for it are

Pottery on Lombok

An elaborate Balinese mask

Traditional weaving

Celuk and Kamasan (near Klungkung). Many silversmiths will make jewellery to order, though it may take a few days to produce.

Shadow play figures, usually made of buffalo leather, are popular souvenirs. Caution is required, however: often high prices are asked for figures which are said to be old, but most pieces are not nearly so old as they are claimed to be, having been subjected to an artificial ageing process. This does not reduce their exotic charm, but it does not justify the high price asked.

Shadow play figures

Rattan and bamboo furniture is made in Mas. It can be ordered from the catalogue and will then be shipped (at high cost) to anywhere in the world. Prospective purchasers should check that the material has been treated for protection against insect attack.

Bamboo furniture

In addition to textiles, the craftsmen of Lombok produce attractive pottery.

Pottery

See entry

Antiques

Sightseeing Flights

To get a bird's eye view of Bali from a helicopter is an attractive (though expensive) possibility. Apply to:

Heli Tour and Spot Charter Service
Asahi Airways, Ngurah Rai Airport (Denpasar)
Tel. 754952 or 751011, ext. 3116

Motive Bali Tours and Travel
Jalan Bypass Ngurah Rai (Denpasar). Tel. 289018

Social Etiquette

Tolerant as the Asian peoples are of the manners of their western visitors, there are certain forms of conduct which disturb even the proverbial equanimity of the Balinese. Even though he may not be aware of it, a visitor behaving in an unacceptable way has lost face and with it the respect of the Balinese.

Ordinary politeness requires a photographer to ask permission before photographing or filming anyone. Usually a gesture with the camera will be enough.

Photography

Conversations should be conducted with polite reserve. Violent gesticulation, or even pointing a finger at other people, is regarded as unseemly. Even between friends intimate subjects are not usually discussed: questions about your income or personal situation, for example, should be answered evasively. Conversation should always be carried on with a smile; the more non-committal the answer, the friendlier the smile.

Conversation

If you are invited into a Balinese family compound it is usual to offer a small gift. The lady of the house will be delighted to receive a bunch of flowers; if there are children sweets are always acceptable. Before entering a house you should take off your shoes.
For a visit to any official agency a shirt and respectable shoes are essential: hippie-like dress is frowned on.

Visits

Taboos

The left hand is regarded as unclean, and should not be used either for offering or receiving anything.

Public displays of affection are unseemly. Nude bathing is offensive to Balinese feelings and is prohibited.

Climbing on temple walls or figures is strictly forbidden and attracts heavy fines. This is an offence which presents the Balinese with almost insoluble problems, for a temple which has been desecrated in this way has lost much of its spiritual character.

At certain points during temple festivals the taking of a flash photograph may arouse intense irritation among the worshippers. It is difficult to lay down rules of behaviour, since attitudes may differ from village to village and from temple to temple; but in these circumstances permission should always be asked before taking any photographs. It goes without saying that great discretion should be used in photographing any religious activity.

Sacrilege

It is strictly forbidden for anyone with an open wound, or for women during menstruation, to enter a temple. Any infringement of this rule amounts to sacrilege: the temple would have been desecrated and would have to be re-sanctified by elaborate rituals.

For visits to temples and attendance at religious ceremonies correct dress is essential: shorts and T-shirts are frowned on. Within the precincts of a temple a selendang (temple shawl or scarf) must be worn. At temple festivals the wearing of a sarong by both men and women (including visitors) is obligatory. Sarongs can be hired at the entrance to a temple for a small charge

Protection of the environment

See Facts and Figures, Protection of Nature and the Environment

Women travellers

See entry

Sport

In the large hotels on Bali and Lombok there are facilities for a variety of sports and recreations, sometimes with staff to organise them.

In any sporting activity, particularly a strenuous one, the early morning or late afternoon should be avoided. Adequate protection against the sun is essential.

Surfing

The Balinese coasts offer great opportunities for experienced surfers. Surfboards can be hired locally. Beginners should pay heed to the advice of local people, since at some points round the coasts there are dangerous underwater currents.

Wind-surfing

Only a few stretches of coast are suitable for wind-surfing. Elsewhere high waves and underwater currents make it hazardous. Here again the advice of local people should be heeded.

Diving

Bali is not one of the world's paradises for scuba divers and snorkellers. The underwater world off its coasts has no great surprises to offer; the coral banks have been almost completely destroyed by fishing with the use of dynamite (which is now banned); and the water is often clouded. The best time to go diving is the early morning.

Some hotels in Nusa Dua, Sanur and Kuta and at Senggigi Beach on Lombok have diving centres where equipment can be hired. It is also possible during a holiday on Bali to gain the internationally recognised PADI certificate after completing a basic training course in diving.

There are good diving grounds at Sanur, Nusa Dua, Padang Bai, Tulamben, Gili Toapekong, Amed and Singaraja-Lovina and round the islands of Menjangan and Penida. With a little luck you may come upon an anglerfish, of which there are said to be some particularly fine specimens round Bali. A "loner" which is often found on coral banks and reefs, it can reach a length of 30 cm (12 in.) and is able to adapt its colour and appearance to its surroundings.

For information apply to:

Bali Marine Sports
Jalan Bypass Ngurah Rai, Blanjong, Denpasar
Tel. 288776
Booking office: Hotel Club Bualu Nusa Dua Bali, tel. 771310/11

P. T. Wisata Tirta Baruna (Baruna Water Sports)
Jalan Bypass I Gusti Ngurah Rai, Denpasar
Tel. 7512236
Baruna Water Sports has booking offices in some of the larger hotels on Bali and in the large hotel at Senggigi Beach on Lombok.

Diving excursions (one or more days; experienced divers only) in the two-masted barque "Golden Hawk" are run by:

Golden Hawk Cruises
Jalan Danau Poso 20 A, Sanur
Tel. 287431

At Nusa Dua, on the Bukit Badung peninsula, within easy reach of the large international hotels, is an 18-hole golf course of great scenic beauty laid out by the Balinese tourist authorities. It is open to all on payment of the appropriate green fee. Caddies are available, and clubs can be hired. Information from hotel reception desks.

Golf

Golf course, Nusa Dua

There are also golf courses at Ubud and Bedugul, and others are planned, some of them in association with new hotels.

Tennis Many of the international hotels (see entry) have tennis courts (sometimes with floodlighting). There are coaches and ball boys if required.

Riding Pony trekking (half-day or whole-day trips, including trips going inland from the coast) is run by:

P. T. Bali Jaran Jaran Kencana
Loji Gardens Hotel, Legian
Tel. 751672 and 751746

Other sports In some of the larger hotels there are fitness centres offering a varied range of sports and recreations (table tennis, volleyball, football, gymnastics, sauna, steam baths, etc.).

Taxis

See Public Transport

Telephones, Telegrams, Fax

See Postal and Telephone Services

Television

See Radio and Television

Time

Indonesia extends over three time zones. Bali and Lombok observe Central Indonesian Standard Time, 8 hours ahead of Greenwich Mean Time.
There is no Summer Time in Indonesia.

Calendar systems See Calendars

Tipping

Although in most restaurants and hotels the bill includes a service charge of 5–10 per cent, it is usual, if the service has been satisfactory, to add a tip or to round up the amount of the bill. Porters and chambermaids in a hotel should be given a small tip at the beginning of your stay and, if you are satisfied with the service, another when you leave.
Taxi-drivers and drivers of buses and bemos do not normally get a tip.

Toilets

Visitors to Bali will still encounter, particularly in country areas, the "squatting" type of lavatory, the use of which calls for a certain degree of skill. Toilet paper is rarely supplied: normally you will find only a tub of water with a dipper.
Public lavatories, where they exist, are identified by the sign "Kamar

Kecil". The sign for men's lavatories is "Laki", for women's "Perempuan".

In the larger hotels and restaurants patronised by westerners there are lavatories of normal western type.

Travel Agencies

In Denpasar, Kuta, Legian, Sanur and Ubud there are numerous travel agencies which offer excursions into the interior of the island and will often book air tickets or confirm your return flight.

Travel Documents

All visitors to Indonesia must have a passport valid for at least six months from the date of arrival. Citizens of the United Kingdom and other European Union countries, Australia, New Zealand, the United States and Canada do not require a visa for a stay of up to two months if they are visiting as tourists and staying in hotel-type accommodation. This period cannot be extended without a visa.

Passport

Visitors must also be able to show that they have a ticket for their return home or onward passage by air or sea.

It is advisable to make photocopies of these documents and carry them separately from the documents themselves. The copies will make it easier to obtain replacements if the originals are lost or stolen.

Visitors arriving in Indonesia from western countries do not at present require a certificate of inoculations unless they have travelled through an infected zone – i.e. various African countries, India, Nepal, Myanmar (Burma), Sri Lanka (Ceylon), etc. Information about current regulations can be obtained from an Indonesian embassy or consulate. Proof of smallpox vaccination (not more than three years old) will probably continue to be required even after the World Health Organisation has declared the world smallpox-free.

Inoculations

Immunisation against cholera and a prophylactic course of anti-malaria pills are advisable for visits outside the tourist areas or during the rainy season.

See Car Rental

Driving licence

When to Go

The best time to visit Bali is between May and September, when rainfall is at its lowest (under six days with rain per month). This is the result of the south-eastern monsoon which blows up from Australia, bringing with it maximum day temperatures of around 30°C (86°F). The months of June and July are regarded as cool, since day temperatures rise to no more than 26°C (79°F). The hot days are best spent in the cooler upland regions, where refreshing winds make the temperature tolerable.

The high season on Bali is from the beginning of June to the beginning of September. Many visitors, particularly from neighbouring countries, also come during the Christmas holidays.

The western monsoon blows from October to April/May, bringing rain – sometimes abundant rain. Although these months are called the rainy season, this does not mean that it rains all day: the rain usually falls only during the night or early morning, when it can be very heavy, but later

The scenery of Bali is still beautiful in the off-season

in the day the clouds disappear and the sky is blue again. During this off-season Bali and Lombok are quieter, there are more empty rooms in the hotels and it may be possible to get reductions on their tariffs.

See also Facts and Figures, Climate.

Women Travellers

Women travelling on their own are unlikely to be troubled by Balinese men, but must expect to be the target of attentions from male visitors. They should take the obvious precaution of not going for walks by themselves in lonely or broken country, particularly after dark.

See also Dress, Emergencies

Young People's Accommodation

In addition to its hotels Bali has other types of accommodation which will appeal particularly to low-budget travellers – "homestays", "losmens" and "penginapans". In these establishments, which rarely have single rooms – more usually two or more beds to a room – the cost of a night's lodging is likely to range between £4 ($6) and £10 ($15), which may include a simple breakfast. Booking in advance is advisable at any time of year.

Index

209

Index

Principal Sights of Tourist Interest

Imprint

147 illustrations, 5 situation plans, 5 drawings, 4 town plans, 3 general maps, 3 temple plans, 2 maps of islands, 2 tables, 1 ground-plan, 1 large map of Bali.

Original German text: Heiner Gstaltmayr

Editorial work: Baedeker-Redaktion

General direction: Dr Peter H. Baumgarten, Baedeker Stuttgart

Cartography: Franz Kaiser, Sindelfingen; Gert Oberländer, Munich; Archiv für Flaggenkunde Ralf Stelter, Hattingen; MapSys GmbH, Kandel/Pfalz (large map of Bali)

Source of illustrations: Amberg (9), Archiv für Kunst und Geschichte (1), Baedeker-Archiv (1), Beck (1), Boyke (2), dpa (1), Garuda Indonesia Airlines (1), Gstaltmayr (114), Historia-Photo (1), Mauritius (3), Strobel (4)

Front cover: Tony Stone Images. Back cover: AA Photo Library (B. Davies)

3rd English edition 1999

Published by AA Publishing (a trading name of Automobile Association Developments Limited, whose registered office is Norfolk House, Priestley Road, Basingstoke, Hampshire RG24 9NY. Registered number 1878835).

Distributed in the United States and Canada by:
Fodor's Travel Publications, Inc.
201 East 50th Street
New York, NY 10022

Licensed user:
Mairs Geographischer Verlag GmbH & Co.
Ostfildern-Kemnat bei Stuttgart

Printed in Italy by G. Canale & C. S.p.A., Turin

ISBN 0 7495 2049 3

Notes

Notes

Klungkung still paint: see Art and Culture, Painting) relate a whole story in a series of scenes in which the same person always features. Among the scenes depicted are the heaven which will reward those who observe law and order in their lives and the punishments which await sinners. An offender being tried in the Court Hall had only to raise his head to get a rather alarming idea of the penalties to which he might be subjected.

The paintings are in five basic colours – yellow, red, blue, black and white.

In the centre of the hall are a rectangular table and six chairs for the three judges, who were priests (*pedanda*), and the assessors.

Surroundings

The village of Kamasan, 2 km (1¼ mi.) south of Klungkung, is noted for its painters, who work in the traditional wayang technique, and its excellent goldsmiths and silversmiths (whose products can be purchased). **Kamasan**

2 km (1¼ mi.) beyond Kamasan is Gelgel. Nothing is left of the former splendour or the buildings of the old town, once a place of considerable consequence. **Gelgel**

A few kilometres from Klungkung on the road to Amlapura lies the little coastal village of Kusamba, whose inhabitants live mainly by fishing and salt production. On the way there traces of the violent volcanic eruption of 1963 can still be seen. **Kusamba**

Krambitan

See Tabanan, Surroundings

Kubutambahan   L 1

Region: North Bali
District: Buleleng
Altitude: sea level

By road: from Singaraja east in direction of Amlapura. Access
Bus and bemo: good services from Singaraja.

The town of Kubutambahan lies 12 km (7½ mi.) north of Singaraja in an alluvial plain which in spite of its low rainfall is intensively cultivated (coffee, maize).

Kubutambahan is a typical northern Balinese town. The townscape, being modern, is of no particular interest.

Sights

The Pura Meduwe Karang is a Hindu temple dedicated to the male counterpart of the rice goddess Dewi Sri. The name of the temple means "to whom the earth belongs", and the local people come here to beg for a rich harvest in the surrounding coffee, maize, fruit and vegetable plantations. ★★Pura Meduwe Karang

The temple consists of three parts. In the first courtyard (jaba) are three platforms, with 13 figures in the lowest row, ten in the middle row and 13 in the rear row. All the figures represent characters from the "Ramayana".

A four-tiered split gate (*candi bentar*) leads into the second courtyard (*jaba tengah*). On the rear wall, which lies between this courtyard and the third one (jeroan) containing the holy of holies (*bebaturan*), are a whole series of figures.

In the centre of the third courtyard is a square stepped platform on which are, to the left, a *gedong pesimpangan* dedicated to Ratu Ayu Sari (a manifestation of the earth mother Ibu Prtiwi), and to the right the *gedong pesimpangan* of Ratu Ngurah Sari, protector of the produce of the earth.

Of particular interest is a relief on the right-hand side of the central platform, showing a man on a bicycle, the wheels of which are decorated with flowers. Although the local people believe that this carving is at least 400 years old, it is thought that the figure on the bicycle represents the Dutch ethnologist W. O. J. Nieuwenkamp, who rode on a bicycle (a means of transport previously unknown to the local people) when working in northern Bali around 1904. The relief is not now in its original condition: it was badly damaged in the 1917 earthquake and was altered during the process of restoration.

Sambiran

25 km (15 mi.) east of Singaraja, at the village of Pacung, a road goes off on the right to Sambiran. The people of this little village believe that they are descended from the Bali Aga, the original inhabitants of Bali; and indeed they speak a dialect which is close to Old Javanese. A further distinctive characteristic is their method of disposing of the dead: while elsewhere on Bali (with the exception of Trunyan: see Penelokan, Surroundings) the dead are cremated, the people of Sambiran throw the bodies of the dead into a gorge at some distance from the village.

There are a number of temples in the village, but all of them are modern.

Kuta

See Denpasar, Surroundings

Legian

See Denpasar, Surroundings

Lombok

Province (of Indonesia): Nusa Tenggara Barat
Area: 4695 sq. km (1812 sq. mi.)
Altitude: 0–3726 m (12,225 ft)
Population: about 2.4 million
Chief town: Mataram

Lombok ("Isle of Chillies") is an island in the Lesser Sundas, Bali's nearest neighbour to the east. Bali and Lombok have been described as sister islands, but they are sisters very different from one another: while Bali is an internationally known holiday island, Lombok remained until quite recently almost unknown, visited only by backpackers and described by those familiar with the region as "Bali as it used to be". It seems that this situation is about to change, for the international hotel